Learning First!

In our work together over the past five years, we have learned firsthand
about the commitment of urban educators. Seeing their dedication and the price they pay
every day, we are overwhelmed with admiration and the sense of a shared struggle. At times the violence
poverty, racism, and just plain human degradation that impact some of our children affect
the entire school. The commitment of urban educators, students, and parents
gives us hope that over time their struggle will make a difference.

Learning First!

A School Leader's Guide to
Closing Achievement Gaps

Carolyn J. Kelley

James J. Shaw

CORWIN
A SAGE Company

For information:

Corwin
A SAGE Company
2455 Teller Road
Thousand Oaks, California 91320
(800) 233-9936
Fax: (800) 417-2466
www.corwinpress.com

SAGE Ltd.
1 Oliver's Yard
55 City Road
London EC1Y 1SP
United Kingdom

SAGE India Pvt. Ltd.
B 1/I 1 Mohan Cooperative
Industrial Area
Mathura Road, New Delhi 110 044
India

SAGE Asia-Pacific Pte. Ltd.
33 Pekin Street #02-01
Far East Square
Singapore 048763

Printed in the United States of America.

Library of Congress Cataloging-in-Publication Data

Kelley, Carolyn (Carolyn Jean)
Learning first! : A school leader's guide to closing achievement gaps/Carolyn J. Kelley, James J. Shaw.
        p. cm.
Includes bibliographical references and index.
ISBN 978-1-4129-6696-2 (cloth)
ISBN 978-1-4129-6697-9 (pbk.)
    1. Academic achievement . 2. Motivation in education. 3. Educational leadership.
4. Educational change. 5. Cognitive learning. I. Shaw, James J. II. Title.

LB1062.6.K45 2009
371.2'03—dc22   2009023355

This book is printed on acid-free paper.

09   10   11   12   13   10   9   8   7   6   5   4   3   2   1

Acquisitions Editor:	Debra Stollenwerk
Associate Editor:	Julie McNall
Production Editor:	Eric Garner
Copy Editor:	Jeannette McCoy
Typesetter:	C&M Digitals (P) Ltd.
Proofreader:	Theresa Kay
Indexer:	Molly Hall
Cover Designer:	Karine Hovsepian

Contents

Table of Cases

Table of Tools

Preface

Diversity is the greatest strength of public schools, and their greatest challenge. As the country has grown more diverse, many communities have divided themselves based on race, diversity, culture, and language. But public schools provide opportunities for students from different cultural, economic, and social backgrounds to work side by side, excel, and appreciate one another's strengths and weaknesses, similarities and differences. This exposure has the potential to broaden student understanding and overcome prejudice based on race, (dis)ability, culture, or family background. More important, diverse learning environments have the potential to accelerate learning for all students (Darling-Hammond, 2007). And yet, few public schools have been successful in overcoming obstacles to learning associated with poverty and diversity. Significant gaps in learning opportunities and outcomes persist and adversely impact all of us.

The premise of this book is that school leaders can significantly raise student achievement and successfully overcome opportunity gaps. Addressing achievement gaps and significantly advancing learning for all students is not only possible, it is a moral and economic imperative.

A departure from a checklist of popular interventions, this book describes the findings from an intensive process of documenting mastery in leadership practice undertaken by the University of Wisconsin–Madison between 2002 and 2008. During that time, we sought input from hundreds of educational leaders, reviewed research on educational leadership, examined the contents of the few professional development programs that exist for master educational leaders in the United States and England, and worked intensively with about 75 principals and district administrators responsible for significantly advancing equity in student learning in their schools and districts.

Throughout this process, we worked to refine a definition of mastery in educational leadership, including consideration of work done by numerous highly skilled scholars in the field, who have themselves defined various xii • Learning First!

forms and characteristics of expert educational leadership. These scholars have advanced notions of instructional leadership, distributed leadership, trust, integrity, credibility, reciprocal or transformational leadership, and moral leadership, including a focus on leaders' internal decision-making structures and the ways in which they relate to others.

Our goal was to describe the ways in which leaders significantly improve the performance of students in their schools, including closing achievement gaps among diverse student groups. Looking across schools, we found common themes in the ways leaders approach decision making; the ways they motivate and engage teachers, staff, students, parents, and community members around a clear and focused goal of high-level learning outcomes for all students; the ways they create energy and enthusiasm for collaborative learning among staff; and the ways they focus their work. There were important differences in context that leaders had to be responsive to, including the length of time the leader had spent in the school, the history of the school, resource levels, teacher and student demographics, and level of community support for and involvement in education. These context factors shaped leader behaviors, educational interventions, and political dynamics in important ways. Despite these important differences, there were clear themes in the ways school leaders approached the work of significantly improving student learning. We believe these approaches can be readily learned and applied to any educational setting to make significant improvements in learning outcomes. (In fact, the principals we describe reflect good leadership practice in any learning organization, not just in schools.) In short, they describe an approach to mastery in educational leadership that can provide a guide for leader preparation and development. Even the master principals we worked with extended and strengthened their practice by documenting and reflecting on their work using the *Learning First* framework.

This work reflects a true marriage of research and practice. We gratefully acknowledge the intellectual contributions of the master administrators who participated in this work with us. Out of our commitment to them, and in gratitude for their willingness to share problems and struggles as well as joys and accomplishments, we have committed to sharing what we learned from them in this volume. They worked to shape and refine our understandings, enabling us to develop this roadmap of leadership for learning.

WHAT IS *LEARNING FIRST* LEADERSHIP?

Broadly, we define educational leadership as the ability to build school or district organizations that produce learning environments in which all students can experience the highest levels of academic success, and the school community strives to continuously improve and meet the needs of all learners. *Learning First* leadership is shared problem solving focused on closing achievement gaps and advancing learning for all students.

Prior research on mastery in educational leadership defines expert leadership as problem solving (Leithwood & Steinbach, 1995). *Learning First* extends this conception of the leader as expert problem solver to leadership as a social process involving shared problem solving in a community of learners. *Learning First* describes the leadership practices of principals who have made quantum improvements in student learning and closed persistent achievement gaps. In our view, much of the leadership literature is devoted to lists of administrator characteristics, principles, and practices intended for universal application. Too often, such principles and practices are applied without careful consideration of the problem and the context.

Learning First leadership is a social process of defining and solving problems that is sensitive to the unique context of a particular school. It is a way of thinking, interacting, and learning. It is shared leadership focused on learning in a community.

Learning First provides educational leaders with a cognitive framework for building communities of practice that strengthen teaching and learning through three related elements:

1. *Socio-Cognitive Leadership* describes the shared cognitive approach to decision making present in schools that have succeeded in closing achievement gaps.

2. *The Dimensions of Leadership for Learning* describe where school leaders focus their attention to move student learning forward.

3. *Levers of Change* describe the individual, organizational, and community levers that master principals use to advance the Dimensions of Leadership for Learning.

At the heart of the model, the leader builds a school community that shares a common approach to problem solving. Socio-Cognitive Leadership provides a cognitive framework shared by the individual leader, the school, and community members that defines, frames, and supports change efforts. Socio-Cognitive Leadership involves building a school community that approaches decision making collaboratively by developing *a shared vision of the preferred state, problem setting with data, identifying evidence-based plans, assessing value-added results,* and *reflecting for continuous improvement.* This is the way Socio-Cognitive Leaders and their learning communities define and solve problems. As Socio-Cognitive

Leaders reflect on their work and self-assess, they examine what value has been added by leadership interventions in terms of student learning gains and other relevant outcomes.

Thus, Socio-Cognitive Leadership relates to key principals of learning, cognition, and motivation: all learning is social (Bandura, 1976; 1997; Vygotsky, Cole, John-Steiner, Scribner & Souberman, 1978; Wertsch, 1985); learning is based on experience (Bransford, Brown, & Cocking, 1999); an engaged community with a shared cognitive framework for moving forward will be motivated to pursue high levels of learning for all students (Wenger, 1998).

School leaders apply Socio-Cognitive Leadership to the four Dimensions of Leadership for Learning: *advancing equity and excellence in student learning, developing teacher capacity, managing and aligning resources,* and *engaging community.* The core dimension is Advancing Equity and Excellence in Student Learning. This dimension focuses the school community on outcomes and helps to define and address existing gaps between the vision for equity and excellence in learning for all students and the current reality. The three process dimensions provide mechanisms to address these learning gaps by focusing on critical dimensions of leadership: improving instruction, acquiring and aligning resources targeted to improve student learning outcomes, and engaging community to support student learning.

The Levers of Change address the social nature of leadership and the interaction between the leader, the school organization, and the larger school community. The Levers of Change highlight the reciprocal nature of leadership and learning. The leader impacts the school and community and is impacted by them. Caring, respectful relationships are needed to support learning. The Levers of Change emphasize building shared understandings, expectations, and commitment to the success of every child.

HOW THIS BOOK IS ORGANIZED

Throughout the book, we provide case examples of schools that have closed achievement gaps to illustrate how school leaders put *Learning First* into practice. We provide tools that school and district leaders can use with their school communities to build shared understandings and advance learning for all students. For each of the four Dimensions of Leadership for Learning, we provide audits with guiding questions that help school communities effectively examine school data and processes and identify areas of focus for improvement efforts. We provide a list of best practices that research evidence—and the experience of our *Learning First* leaders—shows can overcome hurdles to advancing learning for all students. And we provide tools shared by *Learning First* schools that can be used to advance learning for all students.

The book is divided into four sections. Chapters 1 and 2 make up the introduction, which provides a context and overview of the *Learning First* framework. This introduction lays the foundation for the remainder of the book, which provides more detail about the *Learning First* framework, and how to carry it out. This framework enables school leaders to build communities of practice that can work effectively together, focus on dimensions of leadership that improve school effectiveness, and produce significant gains in learning outcomes for all students, including the students who traditionally struggle the most.

We have found the *Learning First* framework to be more powerful than a list of knowledge, skills, and dispositions for principals because it provides guidance on how to approach the role of leader for learning: specifically, how to approach leadership and decision making, where to focus leadership efforts, and what mechanisms are most likely to move change efforts forward. *Learning First* is a systematic approach to leadership grounded in learning theory and leadership practice, focused on the development and use of the learning community as the preeminent strategy for school improvement. It provides clear direction and guiding questions to focus the work of the leaders and emphasizes individual, organizational, and community aspects of moving a change process forward.

Socio-Cognitive Leadership is introduced in Chapter 2 and described more fully in Chapters 3 and 4. Chapters 5 through 8 examine how to advance each of the dimensions of leadership for learning. Throughout the chapters, we provide case examples of master principals and tools that can be used by the leader individually and/or in collaboration with the school community to address specific goals that advance student learning.

Next, we examine three Levers of Change: the individual leader, the school organization, and internal and external community. Chapters 9 and 10 examine the roles of the principal and district in advancing *Learning First* through the Levers of Change and provide example tools that principals and districts can use to support the change process at the individual, organization, and community levels.

The Table of Cases and Table of Tools enable easy reference to the examples and instruments provided throughout the text. In addition, at the end of the text are two resources that summarize the *Learning First* framework. Resource A is a Socio-Cognitive Leadership Rubric that provides a set of questions that focus work on the four Dimensions of Leadership for Learning and a rubric that can be used to formatively assess the implementation of Socio-Cognitive Leadership at the novice, journey, and master levels.

Resource B is a friendly observer site-visit protocol to assist school communities in identifying areas of focus for leadership development and school improvement. Our view is that leadership can only be assessed by understanding the school context and the school community. Leader effectiveness is a reflection of the extent to which members of the school community share a clear vision, understand and use data to address the dimensions of leadership for learning, and pursue evidence-based interventions designed and evaluated to address vision gaps. Thus, we view the site visit as a critical tool to support leadership development and school improvement.

HOW TO USE THIS BOOK

This book is a guide for principals, superintendents, and school communities to close achievement gaps and advance learning for all students. The book is designed to guide principals and leadership teams in the implementation of the *Learning First* framework. After the team works through Chapters 2 through 4 familiarizing themselves with the *Learning First* Framework, Chapters 5 through 8 provide case examples, tools, and resources that enable the team to apply Socio-Cognitive Leadership to the four Dimensions of Leadership for Learning tailored to your individual school context.

Each chapter provides a description of leadership practice that puts learning first and examples of how master principals have applied the framework to advance learning in their schools. Audit tools designed to be tailored to the school's specific context and vision provide guidance on the types of data the team should analyze to clearly define the status quo and identify vision gaps that need to be addressed. Examples of evidence-based practices provide an initial menu of ideas for strategies the school might take to address vision gaps.

As the leadership team works through the model, they should identify strategies for building shared understanding of the model throughout the school community, so that teachers in classrooms see themselves as part of the community of practice committed to advancing learning for all students. From the boardroom to the classroom, members of the school community share a common approach to problem solving that involves establishing a clear vision, defining vision gaps through data analysis, identifying an evidence-based plan that specifically addresses those gaps, assessing value-added results, and reflecting to reframe the vision or plan for continuous improvement.

A second use of this book is for districts to build the leadership of their principals. This book would be an excellent book study for a team of principals from across the district. The team could work together to apply the *Learning First* framework districtwide and work through an initial application of the framework to their own individual school data as part of a school improvement planning process, a reflective self-assessment, or to establish individual leadership goals for themselves and their school communities. The book could also be used as a manual for a leadership development program for all employees including school and district-level administrators, school board members, teachers, and teaching support staff.

Resource A at the end of the book provides a rubric for formative assessment of schools and school leadership, which can be used by the principal, the school leadership team, the district, or by a team of friendly observers to provide feedback and strengthen principal leadership. A template and description of a friendly observer site-visit process is described fully in Resource B.

Finally, this book provides an excellent resource as a text in leadership preparation programs for school and district leaders. It brings together in one place a clear, cognitive approach to the principalship, emphasizing important features of strong leadership that focus and build a shared approach to problem solving and target the efforts of the individual leader, the school, and the community. For a beginning principal or as professional development for an experienced principal, the model guides and focuses principal leadership practice.

Throughout, the book provides a clear description of how to embark on a school improvement process that builds and engages the school and community to put learning first. Our premise, consistent with our research in schools and our work with master principals, is that school communities, focused on learning and shared leadership, hold high expectations and achieve high outcomes for all students. Through focused analysis of data and strident commitment to the vision of learning for all, they succeed in meeting the nation's moral commitment to all learners by closing achievement gaps and producing quantum improvements in teaching and learning for all students.

Acknowledgments

The premise of this book is that schools are most effective when groups of committed individuals share a vision for excellence and work together in a community to advance that vision. Similarly, this book is the result of the collective experience and social interactions of literally hundreds of educational leaders, including principals, teachers, parents, community members, central office administrators, superintendents, researchers, professors, graduate students, and policymakers. Writing and developing the ideas in this book has been the most intensive learning experience of our lives. The intensity emanates from engaging the commitment of talented, motivated educational leaders who recommit themselves every day to ensure that all children—regardless of their learning styles, personality, history, family background, or circumstance—are provided an effective learning environment that enables them to be challenged, engaged, and successful. These leaders share a commitment and a passion for all children. Where others may see barriers, they see opportunities for learning.

Although this book is a pale reflection of the energy, commitment, and talent of the folks we have worked with, we hope that we have captured the essence of their work so that others can join us on a critical journey to improve the quality of educational opportunities for all students and end what Jonathan Kozol has termed *educational apartheid* in America. No matter what our skin color, cultural heritage, or economic circumstance, our collective fates as Americans remain intertwined, and we can only succeed as a country if we are able to build schools that are committed to ensuring that all children succeed.

Corwin gratefully acknowledges the contributions of the following reviewers:

Mary B. Herrmann
Superintendent of Schools
Winnetka Public Schools
Winnetka, IL

About the Authors

 **Carolyn J. Kelley** is a Professor of Educational Leadership and Policy Analysis at the University of Wisconsin–Madison. She is an internationally recognized scholar in teacher compensation policy whose research focuses on the preparation and professional development of school leaders and teacher evaluation and compensation as elements of strategic human resource management in schools. Her current research attempts to build a shared conception of mastery in educational leadership by examining the practices of principals who have closed achievement gaps and significantly improved learning for all students. Through this work, she seeks to build formative assessment tools and intervention strategies to improve leadership practice in schools. Professor Kelley earned her PhD from Stanford University (1993) and conducted research with the Consortium for Policy Research in Education (CPRE) from 1989 to 2002. Her publications include over 30 journal articles, book chapters, and research reports, and she is the coauthor of two books: *Learning First! A School Leader's Field Guide to Closing Achievement Gaps* (with James J. Shaw; Corwin, 2009) and *Paying Teachers for What They Know and Do: New and Smarter Compensation Strategies to Improve Schools* (with Allan Odden; Corwin, 1997 and 2001). She has provided consulting services to numerous states, school districts, and policy and practitioner organizations, including national and state teacher unions.

 **James J. Shaw** is a highly acclaimed educator and administrator in K–12 public education. He served as an educational leader and superintendent of schools for more than thirty years. He is a former Wisconsin Superintendent of the Year and has been recognized by numerous organizations, including the National Education Association, the Saturn

Corporation, and the University of Wisconsin, for his leadership and contributions to public education on the state and national level. He is currently Superintendent of Schools in the Racine Unified School District, a diverse urban district of approximately 2,100 students. He is deeply and directly engaged in the daily challenges of leadership to close achievement gaps and dramatically improve learning in the public schools. He earned his PhD at the University of Wisconsin–Madison (1990). For six years, he served as the Clinical Professor and Director of the Wisconsin Idea Executive PhD Program in the Department of Educational Leadership and Policy Analysis at the University of Wisconsin–Madison. His major work at the university was designing leadership development programs and creating partnerships in K–16 education that promote the integration of theory, research, and practice. His research interests are social learning and learning theory as it relates to school leadership and the development of communities of practice as a central school reform strategy. He is the author of several articles on school leadership and leadership development.

PART I

Introduction

The Case for *Learning First*

I feel an incredible moral imperative for making a difference in our schools. I feel like we are nearing a tipping point, and if things don't change soon, our institutions are going to crumble.

—Sheila Briggs, Elementary School Principal

DON'T ALL SCHOOLS PUT LEARNING FIRST?

"All children can learn."

"No Child Left Behind."

"There are no excuses for poor achievement."

These phrases have been so overused as to become trite, and yet the challenge of leading schools that promote learning for all remains elusive and daunting. The premise of this book is that we must—and we can—dramatically improve student learning, and the way to do that is to make closing achievement gaps and significantly advancing learning for all the top priority of the school community.

You might ask, "Isn't learning the top priority of every school community?" The answer, of course, is "Yes . . . and no."

All schools want the best for their children. They want school staffs to have work environments that are positive and supportive. Schools hire the best teachers they can find, invest in teacher professional development, select curricula that meet their needs, and encourage and reward students for doing well.

But in most schools, the focus on learning is constrained by limits on student motivation and preparation for learning, family and community support for education, resource levels, teacher motivation and skill, contractual obligations, time constraints, and a host of competing goals and values around areas such as citizenship, health and wellness, safety, tradition, and investment in gifted and talented learners. School leaders are evaluated and rewarded for keeping the school safe and orderly, maintaining traditional centers of excellence, and minimizing disruption and complaints.

In addition, the demands of the principal's role and the constant parade of problems that present themselves make it difficult for principals to be proactive. Very few principals consider their work to reflect the focus on instructional leadership they would like it to have if it weren't for all those other demands on their time.

Sometimes, for seemingly good reasons, principals don't focus on putting learning first. Not all educators, parents, or citizens welcome the call for dramatic improvement in learning. In schools where the majority of students are succeeding by traditional measures, efforts to shore up the learning of low-performing students may be viewed as unrealistic and threaten existing values, beliefs, and practices that the school community has come to be proud of. Furthermore, to some, demands for improved performance suggest too much emphasis on test scores, which may ultimately mean less authentic learning for both struggling students and students who are currently succeeding. They fear an emphasis on rote learning and test preparation and the elimination of high-level curricula, such as Advanced Placement courses or music and art programs for gifted students. For these individuals, an over-reliance on test scores threatens to impede the complex intellectual and social development of children.

While we acknowledge these constraints and competing values and commitments, we believe putting learning first is a moral and economic imperative. Even a cursory look at the growing demographic diversity in America and the consistent failure of American schools to meet the educational needs of diverse learners suggest that the future of our country is dependent on our ability to make learning for all the top priority of public schools.

As the diversity in the country reaches half of the workforce, schools will have to make quantum improvements in the learning of minority and low-income students if the country is to remain globally competitive and maintain a strong middle class. In the next section, we describe the changing demographics of the country, the struggles schools have in meeting the needs of the growing body of diverse learners, and the imperative for leadership that puts learning first.

AMERICA'S CHILDREN AND THE MORAL IMPERATIVE FOR *LEARNING FIRST*

America's children are diverse. They are rich and poor; black, brown, and white; accomplished and struggling. They are the children of immigrants, of slaves, and of Native Americans. Children in America have always been diverse in race, cultural background, socioeconomic level, educational experience, and special learning needs. The longstanding diversity of America's children has been reflected in public schools and contributed to the conceptualization of public education as a cultural melting pot and the ladder to citizenship and full economic participation in the American Dream. But the ladder isn't working for all of America's children. Many children are being left behind. Some do not learn, and many are not challenged. In America, the achievement gaps associated with children of color and poverty receive limited attention from the public, but they should be the shame of our nation.

Furthermore, the performance of even the best and brightest children is only average when compared with the similar children from other developed nations. In the past fifty years, the mission of many public schools was limited to the sorting of children by race, by socioeconomic level, and ability. While the sorting of children may be consistent with America's industrialization in the 20th century, it is inimical to America's globalization in the 21st century. In the last twenty years, both diversity in America and the importance of education have dramatically increased. If the ability to educate *all* children to the highest possible level is the measure of success of public schools (Kelley, 1997), most schools are failing miserably.

CHANGING CHILDREN: DIVERSITY, POVERTY, AND ACHIEVEMENT GAPS

The diversity of America's school children has increased dramatically in the past two decades. In 1988, students of color constituted only 22% of the school population. By 2006, students of color constituted 42% and white students 58% of the school population (National Center for Education Statistics [NCES], 2007). America's children of today are more diverse, and there are more of them. In the past twenty years, the total school-age population has grown by approximately nine million students, while the percentage of white students has declined by a third, and the percentage of students of color has nearly doubled.

Increasing diversity is also evident in the changing family and social backgrounds of public school students. In 1994, 73% of families with children were two-parent married families. Just a short time later in 2005, only 67% of families with children were married couples. Eighty-two percent of all Asian families with children are married couples, but only 36% of black families are led by married couples. Furthermore, 37% of all births are to unmarried women. Twenty percent of enrolled public school children speak a language other than English at home, and 5% have difficulty speaking English (National Center for Education Statistics, 2007).

This racial and cultural diversity and differences in family situations all have important implications for schools and school leadership. Schools desiring to build parental partnerships and engage students in learning face significant challenges in understanding and addressing the needs of students and families in their communities.

Furthermore, the need to be sensitive to differences in student needs based on racial and cultural diversity is compounded by economics. Poverty has long been viewed as an educational as well as an economic problem that impacts America's children. Students living in poverty are more likely to experience health and dental problems, have poor school attendance due to illness, and be victims of crime and violence. Students living in poverty are less likely to have health insurance, receive regular health and dental care, and have proper nutrition. For example, only 48% of poor students ages two to four have seen a dentist, and 23% have untreated dental cavities. Poor students are less likely to have parents who are college graduates or enjoy educational resources (books, computers, musical instruments) in the home or experiences (educational trips, visits, activities) associated with educational success (NCES, 2007; Rothstein, 2004).

Research has suggested that growing up in poverty can negatively impact children's mental and behavioral development as well as their overall health. Developmental differences require schools to differentiate curriculum and instruction so that children can build successful learning experiences. Such developmental differences are frequently reported as deficits or learning difficulties (Duncan, Brooks-Gunn, & Klebanov, 1994), and poverty is negatively correlated with long-term educational achievement.

ACHIEVEMENT GAPS

In America, diversity and poverty are frequently associated with lower academic achievement and other measures of performance in public education. In international comparisons, America frequently demonstrates more variation in achievement levels and more inequity in achievement associated with income and diversity than other nations. Significant achievement gaps between whites, blacks, and Hispanics have been documented in the National Assessment of Educational Progress (NAEP) since 1970. Gaps in other performance indicators associated with diversity and poverty are even more startling. According to the Education Trust (2005), young people in America from high socio-economic status (SES) families have a 75% chance of graduating from college, whereas young people from low SES families have only a 9% chance of graduation. Appallingly, the children of rich Americans are *eight times* more likely to graduate from college than children raised in poverty.

In the 2004 NAEP, white students continued to outperform black and Hispanic students in both reading and mathematics, but there is evidence that the achievement gap is closing at the elementary level and that some progress is being made at the middle and high school levels. The score gaps for black, Hispanic, and white students were smaller in 2004 than in the early 1970s (NCES, 2007).

On an international level, U.S. 15-year-olds scored lower than the average on the 2003 Program for International Student Assessment (PISA) mathematics literacy assessment. The U.S. average (483) on the mathematics literacy assessment was lower than the Organization for Economic Cooperation and Development (OECD) average (500). U.S. 15-year-olds scored lower than 20 of the other 28 participating countries and higher than only five countries. The score for white students in the United States was 12 points higher than the OECD average, while the average score for blacks was 83 points lower (NCES, 2007, Dec.).

RESOURCE GAPS

"Savage Inequalities" in educational resources between diverse poor students and majority students have been documented by Kozol (1992) and others (Arroyo, 2008; Darling-Hammond, 2004; Oakes, 1990; Orfield, 2001). Research suggests, "Education outcomes for students of color are much more a function of their unequal access to key educational resources, including skilled teachers and quality curriculum, than they are a function of race" (Darling-Hammond, 2007). In California, according to Darling-Hammond (2007), some high-minority schools are so impoverished that they are forced to shorten school days and the school year, thereby reducing instructional time for the neediest of students. In Wisconsin, we observed high-minority urban schools with more than 35 diverse and poor students in many classrooms, while more affluent suburban schools have average class sizes of less than 25.

Across the country, diverse and poor students are more likely to have untrained, inexperienced, and temporary teachers (Oakes, 1990) and less access to qualified teachers and quality curriculum. Resource gaps are exacerbated by state school-funding systems that are based on local property wealth and permit significant variability in school funding. Nationally, the wealthiest 10% of school districts spend 10 times more per pupil than the poorest 10% (Kozol, 2005). Inequalities also persist within school districts where the schools with the poor and diverse students receive fewer resources than other schools. And within schools, norms of allowing senior teachers to select the *plum* assignments lead to the least experienced teachers frequently being assigned to teach large groups of the neediest students who are tracked and isolated from the larger student population, while highly qualified teachers are assigned to teach small Advanced Placement sections for the more highly motivated *college-bound* students.

LEARNING FIRST!

While it may be argued that academic achievement is strongly impacted by race and class (Rothstein, 2004), schools and school leaders also powerfully impact student achievement by the choices that they make. We believe it is necessary and possible to dramatically increase learning for all students, including those who have traditionally struggled and those who are not challenged. Significant improvement in student performance requires a sustained commitment to increasing access for all students to challenging curriculum and high-quality teaching. African American children, Latino students, English language learners, poor children, special education children, and even our best performing students can learn at higher levels. In international comparisons of student learning, our children should be expected to achieve at least at similar rates as the children of other economically advantaged nations.

In *The School and Society* (1915), John Dewey asserts, "What the best and wisest parent wants for his own child, that must the community want for all of its children" (p. 3). If high-performing students experience rich curriculum and demanding teachers, then struggling students must also experience rich curriculum and demanding teachers. We must want all children to attend safe schools with adequate resources and to graduate prepared for college and careers.

Based on ongoing collaboration with principals who are leading diverse schools to high performance and the documented successes of a growing number of additional schools throughout the country that have closed achievement gaps and strengthened learning outcomes for all students, this book reflects the hope and the realistic expectation that public schools can do much better in educating all children. Many schools currently fail to educate children to their full potential. But the fact that some schools are greatly increasing performance for all students suggests that success is possible for all children and all schools.

Learning First is a call to action for any school leader who feels that learning is compromised by organizational structures and deficit thinking that sorts children rather than challenging them to learn more. Organizational obstacles that sort children by ability are most evident in high schools and urban schools, but urban, suburban, rural, elementary, secondary, and perhaps all schools have pockets of learning inequity and groups of underperforming students. Ever-increasing mounds of achievement data document achievement gaps by gender, race, socio-economic level, and special education need. Variance in learning is expected, but learning prescribed by race or social status suggests that schools could do more to educate diverse children, poor children, and children with special needs.

We do not view education and learning as a zero-sum game in which some can learn more only if others learn less. Schools that put learning first value the success and achievements of all children and increase learning for both the successful and struggling student. Schools alone cannot rectify the long-standing, pernicious social conditions that impact learning, yet a growing body of research on teaching and learning suggests that learning is based on social and cognitive experience, not genetics or social background. If learning is a social cognitive experience, then the more children that learn, the more children will learn. Schools can shape important learning experiences for children and create learning communities that include all students.

Research on how people learn suggests that experience, not ability, is the basis of expertise or learning at high levels. Novice learners become expert learners over time through repeated experiences and reflection that structures experience into meaningful learning. Social learning theory and research suggest that learning is a social phenomenon. Learning is dependent on social interaction and social relationships. Theory, research, and a growing public consensus challenge the notion that only a fortunate few children can succeed as learners or that failure must *be normally distributed*. All children can and need to learn algebra, read quality literature, and write expository essays. We believe *Learning First* principles are both possible and practical: School leaders who learn from experience and the experience of others and build an inclusive community of learners in schools can dramatically improve student learning.

What does it mean to put learning first? In practice, it means that schools make learning the top priority, and they align resources and invest energy in problem solving to advance learning outcomes for students. To understand how schools do this, we conducted research on leaders and schools that made significant progress in one or more core indicators of student learning over a period of three to five years. These leaders were successful in advancing both equity and excellence in student learning. They closed achievement gaps for diverse student populations and accelerated learning for all students. We defined closing achievement gaps in one of two ways. First, achievement gaps are closed when the achievement of diverse students mirrors the achievement of majority students. For example, if 15% of the students in school are African American, at least 15% of the students in Advanced Placement classes are African American. Or second, achievement gaps are closed when schools have achieved rapid and dramatic improvement in student learning for historically lower-achieving students compared to the rate of learning in demographically comparable schools.

Measures of improvement are not limited to test scores. Other measures include student behavior, attendance, graduation, and enrollment in high-level curriculum or extracurricular activities. We define and measure student learning with traditional test scores and with more authentic performance measures such as writing assessments.

Thus, putting learning first means designing and developing public schools that dramatically improve learning for all children regardless of socio-economic background, race, gender, culture, or educational need.

Learning First involves the hard work of improving leadership and teaching practices for all children on a daily basis as the commonsense expression of social justice in America's public schools. It implies results, accountability, high expectations, and dissatisfaction with the status quo. It implies that school leaders and teachers, along with children, families, and communities, have a responsibility for learning outcomes as well as learning opportunities.

Throughout this volume, we describe the ways in which successful schools have dramatically improved student performance by putting learning first. These schools provide vivid examples of leadership that makes a difference. These master school leaders respond to the unique social context of their school community, while sharing a common cognitive roadmap of leadership that advances student learning. This dual emphasis on learning and community, on learning as a social process, and on shared understanding in a unique social context is the core of leadership for learning first. In short, *Learning First* is community learning.

While diversity looks different in different parts of the country, and resource levels to address learning needs vary from state to state and district to district, schools across the nation need to address critical achievement gaps in order for our nation to remain strong and competitive. The achievement gaps in America are invariably associated with diversity and poverty. It is time to stop the finger pointing and begin sharing responsibility and leadership for learning. It is time to put *Learning First* in every school for every child. The remainder of this book focuses on what school leaders can do to overcome these problems. We turn now to lay out a leader's roadmap for putting learning first in schools.

The Roadmap for *Learning First*

While sometimes disagreeing about appropriate solutions to educational problems, educational leaders that close achievement gaps share a common cognitive framework or thought process for addressing problems of practice. This cognitive framework has at its core a clear focus on advancing equity and excellence in learning for all students. The framework can be learned and is adaptable to any educational context. The *Learning First* framework provides a definition of leadership mastery that all educational leaders can use to strengthen their leadership practice. It is grounded in learning theory and has its foundation in the development of communities of practice that work together to continuously improve student learning.

The roadmap, which we refer to as the *Learning First* framework, is illustrated in Figure 2.1. It includes the following three elements:

1. *Socio-Cognitive Leadership*—illustrated in the graphic as the outer ring—defines *What* leadership looks like in schools in which stakeholders share a common approach to analyzing and addressing problems. Specifically, leadership is viewed as a social process that focuses on building communities of practice that share common cognitive frameworks or approaches to decision making and problem solving.

2. *The Dimensions of Leadership for Learning*—depicted as the inner triangle—define *Where* leaders focus their attention in order to close achievement gaps and advance learning for all students.

3. *Levers of Change*—depicted as the three outer rings of the circle to reflect the individual leader, the organization, and the community—show *How* leaders transform schools by focusing on specific strategies or approaches to align the dimension of leadership with the shared vision for advancing student learning.

Figure 2.1   *Learning First* Framework: Leadership as Shared Problem Solving

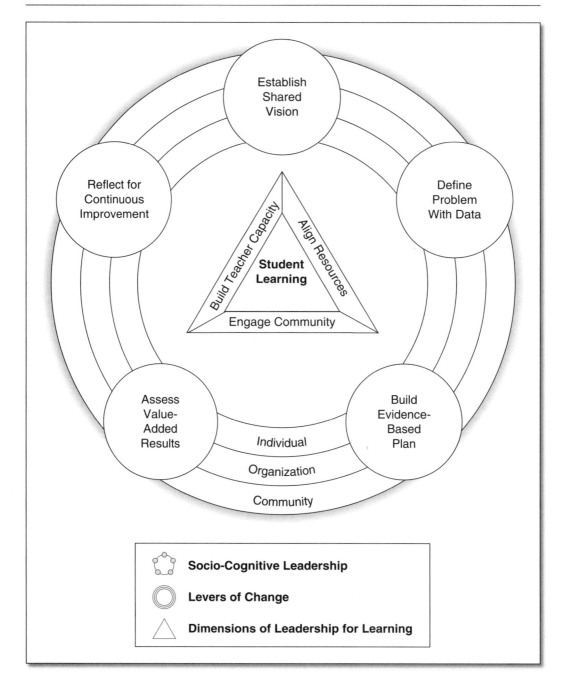

THE SOCIO-COGNITIVE LEADERSHIP PROCESS: THE *WHAT* OF LEADERSHIP FOR LEARNING

Leaders who utilize a *socio-cognitive leadership process* recognize that all learning is social, and in order for schools to move forward as learning organizations, staff and other stakeholders must share a common understanding of how to define and address impediments to student and organizational learning. The process is *socio-cognitive* because it recognizes that *all learning is social* (thus, *socio*), and that for an organization to advance, members of the organization need to share a common vision for the future, a common understanding of the current situation, common tools and strategies for moving forward together, and common metrics for recognizing and assessing performance improvement.

Leadership in this context involves the development of a widely shared vision and agreed-upon methods for understanding and addressing problems of practice. Thus, the *socio*-cognitive leadership process highlights that exceptional school leaders are those that foster *communities* in which stakeholders share a common approach to analyzing and addressing problems. In practice, this means that teachers, staff, and students share a common understanding of the vision, they know how well the school is doing in relation to the vision, and they know the work the school is actively engaged in to advance the vision.

The emphasis on the *cognitive* aspects of leadership highlights that leaders that close achievement gaps and improve learning for all students advance a *cognitive* framework to guide members of the school in identifying and addressing problems of practice. This cognitive framework is consistent with research on effective school leadership, school improvement planning, strategic planning, and evaluation. The decision-making process underlying socio-cognitive leadership advances student learning driven by a clear shared *vision of the preferred state*, a *data profile* or *analysis* that clearly defines or *sets* the problem (Halverson, 2004), the establishment of an *evidence-based plan* to address the problem, analysis of *value-added results* due to the intervention, and *reflection* on the process and outcomes to determine ways to continuously improve to advance learning outcomes.[1]

SHARED VISION OR PREFERRED STATE

The *shared vision* or *preferred state* provides direction and motivates school staff, students, and community members to work together to advance student learning. How is vision-setting different in schools that put learning first? First, the vision reflects a clear and strong focus on *student learning* as the chief priority for the school. It has a moral dimension that describes a compelling purpose and direction for the school that is a call to action for the school's stakeholders. Since it describes what the school could or should be rather than what it is, the vision fosters a shared sense of urgency and dissatisfaction with the status quo. And the vision is collective. It grows out of a common set of core beliefs and the school community holds itself accountable for achieving the vision (Elmore, 2004). Specifically, the vision in learning first schools is based on the following core beliefs:

- All children can learn.
- Learning is social and based on experience.
- Children and adults need a safe, supportive learning environment to be successful.
- The key to advancing student learning is excellence in teaching, which occurs most effectively in strong communities of practice among teachers.
- Effective teaching and learning environments are learner centered, knowledge centered, and assessment centered.

Out of these core beliefs emerges a vision for the school that is shaped and reinforced by the principal through a collaborative process that fosters and supports the establishment of communities of practice among school stakeholders. The vision is not only known by school stakeholders (administrators, teachers, staff, students, parents, volunteers, and community members), but it is embraced by them. They own it.

Vision motivates and directs behavior, and when a vision has a laser-like focus on closing achievement gaps and advancing learning for each child, when it is understood by all and embraced by most, it provides a powerful guiding force for organizational action. In the learning first schools we worked with, the principal and staff had a clear and consistent understanding and could articulate the collective vision of the school.

In these schools, the principal and staff members clearly understand their own core beliefs and how they relate to the collective vision. They understand and can articulate how the vision is lived in the school—how it shapes behavior. And they have a clear understanding of where the school is in relation to the vision, the key opportunities and obstacles the school faces to advance the vision, and the recent history of successes and failures as they relate to the vision. Perhaps most important, the educators in these schools view achievement of the shared vision as a collective moral commitment that the school staff has made to themselves, their students, and their communities.

> ### The Shared Vision or Preferred State
>
> The vision or preferred state...
>
> - Focuses on equity and excellence in student learning as the chief priority of the school
> - Describes a compelling purpose and direction
> - Serves as a call to action
> - Emerges from the leader's core values
> - Is collaboratively developed and widely embraced
>
> Members of the school community hold themselves accountable for achieving the vision

A vision with such power is not created through wordsmithing. Those involved must take time and have a willingness to define, share, and challenge core beliefs; they must have meaningful ongoing conversations about the school and what it could be (not just what it is), including collective analysis of data; and they must establish clear shared expectations to move teaching and learning forward. Thus, the socio-cognitive leadership process begins with the establishment and articulation of a clear shared vision focused on student learning.

DEFINE THE PROBLEM WITH DATA

Closely related to the vision, the next step in the socio-cognitive leadership process is analysis of data, or what we call *problem setting with data*. Socio-cognitive leadership is problem solving, and the first step in problem solving is understanding the problem. "Fire, ready, aim" or implementing best practices irrespective of a well-defined problem will not advance the organization toward the shared vision. Furthermore, a lack of baseline data defining the problem makes evaluation of new practices and strategies impossible. Socio-cognitive leadership defines the problem in relation to the shared vision. The problem is the difference between the present learning condition and the preferred learning condition—what we call the "vision gap." Learning theory suggests that one of the key issues in advancing learning is to overcome prior beliefs, history, and grooves in cognitive maps (Bransford, Brown, & Cocking, 1999). Data analysis provides evidence that describes or sets the problem and establishes the need to set new goals, try new things, and invest time and other resources in moving the organization forward. It can also provide information to inform fine-tuning of instructional practices to sharpen and focus teaching effort so that it is most effective in advancing student learning.

Schools that succeed in advancing equity and excellence in student learning have sophisticated data collection, management, and analysis systems in place. They also have created a culture of reliance on data to inform decision making; teachers crave feedback to sharpen their focus and redirect their work for continuous improvements in teaching and learning. They seek a variety of sources of data beyond state test scores to inform their work. These include diagnostic tests, such as Measures of Academic Progress (MAP; http://www.nwea.org/) or Assessment for Learning and Teaching (ASPIRE; http://www.ascd.org/programs.aspx), student work, and other formal and informal feedback from students, parents, and other sources. In *Learning First* schools, data are widely shared by teachers, administrators, students, parents, and other members of the school community.

Learning First schools establish structures and articulate standards for performance that make data more meaningful and useful for school improvement. Structures could include hiring teacher coaches and providing staff development around analysis and use of data for improving instruction. Data retreats can be a useful tool, but schools that put learning first seek data feedback in daily work and not only as an annual exercise or part of a broader school improvement planning process. For example, Patricia Walsh, the recently retired principal of Earhart Elementary School in Chicago, led the development of schoolwide guidelines for student assignments in math and writing and rubrics to establish clear standards of performance for teachers and students to inform teaching and learning. The schoolwide writing and math prompts and rubrics guide initial instruction to provide assessment feedback on student learning outcomes, which enables teachers to refine and refocus instruction to maintain high expectations and ensure high learning outcomes for all students.

In addition, Principal Walsh personally evaluated one piece of writing from each student each year to support the development of a common metric among teachers across the school for the quality of writing they should expect from students. As a result, Earhart eliminated the racial achievement gap for its 100% African American and 79% poor students. In 2005, 100% of Earhart eighth graders met or exceeded state reading standards (compared to 80% of white students statewide). The school provides rich learning opportunities for its students, anchoring expectations at high levels, and using data to formatively assess teaching and learning and constantly hold students to these high expectations.

Principals in *Learning First* schools model data-based decision making. They establish structures that ensure systematic collection, management, and analysis of data. By comparing the data to the vision, socio-cognitive leaders create a shared sense of dissatisfaction with the status quo. Data analysis enables them to assess progress in achieving the vision and to inform school improvement planning and daily work. While not everyone is involved in schoolwide data analysis, the results of the analysis are widely shared and understood so that school stakeholders are clear about the school's progress in achieving goals and the ways in which data have defined goal targets and informed the choice of interventions to move the school forward.

Define the Problem With Data

The school . . .

- Has a comprehensive process to *collect, manage, and disaggregate data* to advance the vision
- Uses data to *set problems and identify possible causes for gaps between the current reality and the preferred state (vision gaps)*
- Uses data to *assess school strengths and emerging issues*
- Creates a *shared sense of dissatisfaction* with the gaps between the current reality and the preferred state
- Assesses *value added results, compares* to similar schools, and *benchmarks* exceptional practice
- Widely *communicates* the vision gap, which is understood by all

---

DEVELOP AN EVIDENCE-BASED PLAN

The next step in the socio-cognitive leadership process is the development of an evidence-based plan of action. The plan is driven by the vision and the problem as defined by the data profile. Schools that put learning first know exactly why they are pursuing a particular strategy; because they have a clear vision of where they want to be, they have conducted data analysis that tells them exactly what the problems are, and they have identified strategies that have been proven to be successful in addressing these problems in similar schools. Often, plans require tailoring to the specific organizational context. Where the evidence base is weak, the schools develop an intervention and gather data on how well it works and what elements of the strategy are most effective in addressing the defined problem.

Because the vision and the data profiling so clearly focus the school on addressing critical identified learning gaps, teachers understand exactly why they are pursuing this strategy and why the school expects the strategy to work. They know the evidence base for the plan because the strategies and comprehensive action steps chosen to address the goals come from research-based principles of high-performing systems with similar profiles and are directly aligned with the school's own profile and vision. Administrators, teachers, and teacher leaders understand their responsibilities in carrying out the plan because responsibilities are clearly identified and include ways to mobilize the talents of a variety of individuals across the school community.

Thus, the plan clearly lays out the strategies that the school will undertake to advance the vision for student learning. Resources are fully dedicated to the improvement strategies, and additional resources are identified and secured to support implementation of the plan. Virtually all of the *Learning First* schools we have worked with have successfully leveraged significant resources to advance the school improvement plan. These resources include strategic and creative uses of existing school funds, as well as concerted efforts to obtain grants and philanthropic support or to develop other types of entrepreneurial partnerships to invest in the plan.

Develop an Evidence-Based Plan

In the plan, . . .

- *Goals and objectives* are clearly specified, measurable, challenging, and achievable in a specified time
- *Evidence-based strategies* are aligned with the school vision and address the vision gap
- *Leadership responsibilities* are spelled out, opportunities to mobilize others' talents are identified, and resources are acquired and allocated to achieve the plan
- *A systematic assessment* is in place to document and evaluate implementation, baseline measures, and effectiveness defined as the value added by the plan to close achievement gaps

The next step in the socio-cognitive leadership process is assessment of *value-added results.* The plan provides clear direction regarding how results will be assessed, by identifying anticipated outcomes and detailing a systematic and comprehensive effort to assess growth from baseline measures. In addition, the plan includes attention to collecting data about implementation to better inform interpretation of results. Any of a number of factors could keep the intervention from being fully implemented. Needy students could be removed from the intervention for discipline reasons, school supports for teachers may be inadequate, or there could be other things going on in the school that simply competed for time and attention to the plan. Understanding these obstacles can help school communities interpret results and derive appropriate conclusions from the data. But plans for collecting data on program implementation need to occur in the planning phase so that appropriate data are available after the intervention to understand and appropriately interpret results.

ASSESS VALUE-ADDED RESULTS

The fourth cognitive step is assessment of *value-added results* measured by improvements in student learning. *Learning First* schools collect baseline data to assess growth and collect data on a regular basis to assess progress toward goals and benchmarks. Value-added results are analyzed by a subset of the school community, but the entire community understands and can describe the school's progress toward goal achievement.

Analysis of student learning gains is conducted collaboratively by stakeholders and includes a variety of assessment and evaluation measures beyond the required state tests. Teachers and other staff members take ownership for results, and a variety of data sources are analyzed at various levels of the organization to assess individual student progress, classroom (teacher) progress, growth by grade level, and overall school performance improvement. Stakeholders also collect data and analyze stakeholder perspectives on the strengths and limitations of student learning and priorities for improvement.

Measure Value-Added Results

The *results* for student learning . . .

- Are *measured* as *value added* or improvements in learning for each child
- Are *assessed at multiple levels*: the individual student, classroom, grade, school, and community
- Are *benchmarked* against a variety of measures of learning: formative assessments, state test scores, local assessments
- Are *conducted* collaboratively and *can be described by each member of the faculty, staff, and administration*

REFLECTION FOR CONTINUOUS IMPROVEMENT

The last stage of the socio-cognitive leadership process, reflection, is critical for organizational learning or continuous improvement to occur. Here, experience is used to inform future action. The reflection provides a concise but rich assessment of leaders' and others' roles in the improvement effort, strengths, areas for improvement, possible changes, and next steps. Leaders model the values of equity, inquiry, and reflection when answering the questions, "How can I make this better? Where do I go next?"

Reflect for Continuous Improvement

Reflection is the key to continuous improvement and includes the following:

- *Identification of areas* for improvement
- *Assessment of key roles* in the improvement effort
- *A focus on equity and evidence-based practice* when answering, "How can we make this better?" and "Where do we go next?"
- *A systems perspective* that shows integration and connections among improvement efforts and a strong desire for continuous improvement for the organization and the individual

---

The reflection also clearly demonstrates a systems perspective by showing integration and connection among improvement efforts and a strong desire for continuous improvement for the organization and individuals.

THE DIMENSIONS OF LEADERSHIP FOR LEARNING: THE *WHERE*

The second element of leadership for *Learning First* is the dimensions of leadership for learning, or *where* leaders need to focus their attention and effort. The dimensions of leadership include four critical areas of focus for educational leadership to improve student learning. They include the following:

1. *Advancing Equity and Excellence in Student Learning* by closing achievement gaps and advancing learning for all students. This is the core outcome dimension depicted as the center of the triangle with the three process dimensions supporting achievement of the learning goal.

2. *Developing Teacher Capacity* by advancing the abilities of all teachers, including teachers who struggle.

3. *Managing and Aligning Resources* by acquiring and deploying the organization's financial, physical, and human resources to advance student learning.

4. *Building an Engaged Community* by developing and involving internal and external communities to advance student learning.

We turn now to a brief introduction to each of the four dimensions of leadership for learning.

Advancing Equity and Excellence in Student Learning
Guiding Questions

- How have you worked to help students who struggle?
- How have you worked to help students who are not challenged?
- How have you improved access to high-quality teaching and learning for all students?

The core dimension of leadership for learning is *advancing equity and excellence in student learning.* Equity issues exist in every school. Common gaps in performance that occur include systematic differences among subgroups of students in achievement, attendance, discipline, participation in extracurricular activities, and involvement in high-level curriculum.

Thus, advancing equity and excellence in student learning means closing achievement and opportunity gaps and advancing learning for all students. Educational leaders do this by focusing the socio-cognitive leadership process on accelerating learning for students who struggle and students who are not challenged and by continually expanding access to high-quality teaching and learning for all students.

One elementary school we worked with advanced student learning in part by recognizing through data analysis that African American boys were being referred to the office for discipline in much greater numbers than any other group, which effectively reduced their access to quality classroom instruction. In this case, the school developed a new discipline policy that greatly reduced office referrals and expanded access to classroom instruction for all students, including the disproportionately impacted African American males.

In Chapter 5, we provide examples and tools that schools can use to identify the source of equity problems and develop evidence-based solutions so that school policies and structures, teaching, and learning can better focus school resources on addressing learning needs and closing achievement gaps.

Developing Teacher Capacity
Guiding Questions

- How have you worked to build teacher capacity to meet student needs and raise student achievement?
- How have you worked to build a professional learning community with high expectations and accountability for the improvement of teaching and learning?
- How have you worked to support *all* teachers to grow professionally and engage in reflective practice, including teachers who struggle?

Leaders of schools that continuously improve and address the needs of all learners focus much of their leadership effort on ensuring that the school is a learning organization and that a primary area of learning and advancement is the quality of teaching that occurs in the school. These effective leaders continuously strive to grow their human resources through careful hiring, advocating for district resources to support needed staffing, reallocating resources to provide coaching and other professional development opportunities, and providing continuous informal feedback to support teachers to continuously work to hone their teaching skills.

Specifically, three primary areas of focus advance teacher capacity[2]: *advancing pedagogical knowledge* and use of teaching strategies to meet individual student needs and raise achievement levels; *building communities of practice* among teachers to support collaborative problem solving, professional growth, and teacher development; and *working to ensure that all teachers are supported* to grow professionally and engage in reflective practice, including but not limited to the teachers who struggle the most in their teaching practice.

In Chapter 6, we provide examples and tools to help principals work to develop teacher capacity. One case in Chapter 6 illustrates how one principal managed human resources through hiring, professional development, deployment of human resources, advancement of instructional tools for teachers, and the creation of culture of accountability and expectation for learning. The result was that the school more than doubled performance and ultimately 100% of students—from a diverse, low-income community—achieved a proficient score in reading on the state assessment.

Managing and Aligning Resources
Guiding Questions

- How have you aligned all resources (financial, human, and physical resources) to advance the vision of equity and excellence in the school or district?

- How have you acquired and managed resources to address learning inequities in your school or district?
- How have you worked to ensure a safe and secure learning environment for students and staff?

Managing and aligning resources involves *securing, allocating,* and *reallocating financial, physical, and human resources* to address learning inequities in the school. All of the *Learning First* schools we studied and worked with have secured some kind of external financial support. In addition to successful grant writing and fundraising, the principals in these schools develop strong relationships with district personnel and use these connections to obtain support from the district for their work. Chapter 7 provides tools for assessing the allocation of resources and suggests ways to find opportunities to redirect resources to advance student learning.

Leaders in schools that put learning first are also effective managers of physical resources, including facilities management, equipment and supplies, and the allocation and reallocation of space and equipment to address school needs.

In addition, these leaders carefully allocate human resources through scheduling; behavior management; allocation of students to high-quality teachers; and building and engaging parent, volunteer, and community resources. In one case, a school improved student engagement by restructuring the lunch schedule to a single, one-hour period with opportunities for students and teachers to eat lunch and work together in a variety of activities that advance engagement between teachers and students around student learning. This simple reconfiguration of the school day has significantly extended opportunities for informal interaction between teachers and students, scaffolding of learning, and engagement around student and teacher passion for learning.

Building an Engaged Community
Guiding Questions

- How have you worked to understand the community and engage stakeholders in developing and attaining a vision of learning for all students?
- How have you developed internal and external relationships to engage, motivate, and support student learning?
- How have you served as an educational and student advocate in the community?

Community refers to the development of relationships that support student learning at three levels: the *internal community* (teachers, staff, and students), the *immediate external community* (parents, neighbors, school volunteers, and the district office); and the *broader external community* (business organizations, other schools, policymakers, and the professional community). Often, school leaders fail to recognize the importance of the broader external community as a resource, and when they do, they fail to focus this resource effectively to *advance student learning.* Schools that put learning first leverage both internal and external stakeholder support, including financial, political, educational, social, and cultural support, to increase opportunities to motivate and engage students in an active, positive learning community.

Chapter 8 provides tools to help school leaders assess and leverage the capacity of the community to support student learning and provides a case example of a school in a low-income, highly diverse urban community that reached out to the community and used community engagement as a critical element of a successful strategy to advance student learning and close achievement gaps.

LEVERS OF CHANGE: THE *HOW*

As described above, leaders who close achievement gaps and advance learning for all students share a common approach to decision making and focus on the four dimensions of leadership for learning. This section focuses on the third critical element: the specific levers of change that enable exceptional school principals to move an organization by making learning a *social* process. These levers of change occur at the individual leader level, the organizational level, and the community level.

At the *individual level,* the leader enacts and refines the vision through a clear sense of *moral purpose.* Clarity of moral purpose helps to shape leadership behavior; provides an internal compass that directs, motivates, and sustains the principal; and motivates and shapes attitudes and behaviors of teachers, staff, students, parents, and community members (Sergiovanni, 2004, 2006). The shared sense of purpose and direction is communicated both directly, through restatement of the vision, and indirectly, as the principal draws attention to the vision *symbolically* through storytelling, actions, behaviors, attitudes, and artifacts (Deal & Peterson, 2003).

Master principals are also *expert problem solvers* and able to adeptly navigate complex and difficult problems—what Leithwood, Begley, and Cousins (1994) characterize as *swampy* problems. Reviewing a series of studies on mastery in the principalship, Leithwood et al. (1994)

Levers for Change

- *The Individual Leader*
  - Moral leadership
  - Symbolic leadership
  - Expert problem solving
- *The Organizational System*

  - The School
    - Organizational structure
    - Human resources
    - Collaborative problem solving

  - District Support
    - Integration and advancement of district goals
- *The External Community*
  - The local community
  - The professional community of educators
  - The broader policy community

identify differences between expert and nonexpert principals in terms of the following:

- *Goals*: Expert principals adopt a broader range of goals and are more likely to value knowledge over feelings; they also see more complex connections between problems and their impact on student learning.
- *Principles and values*: Expert principals are much more explicit about principles and values in their work.
- *Constraints*: Expert principals are more likely to believe that constraints in problem solving can be overcome.
- *Solution processes*: Experts are more likely to engage in planning and consultation with others and view information gathering as a key problem-solving process.
- *Affect*: Expert principals are calmer in the process of problem solving.

In summary, expert problem solvers exhibit a higher degree of *cognitive flexibility* and a more sophisticated use of *collaboration* with others to identify and solve problems.

At the *organizational-systems* level, expert principals leverage and influence *organizational structures and policies.* Consistent with an *open systems* concept (Scott, 2002), we conceptualize school organizations to have permeable boundaries and fluid membership, including staff on the school payroll as well as a host of volunteers and stakeholders whose time and attention varies considerably at any single point in time. Individuals engage and disengage from the system for a variety of reasons depending on the decision locus and problem context. Thus, parents, extended family members, community members, researchers, district staff, policymakers, police, social workers, health care officials, and others may at any single point in time be considered members of the school organization. Leadership mastery thus involves the ability to structure this amorphous and evolving community into *collaborative, problem-solving* communities of practice (Wenger, 1998) that are focused on problems of learning and are collaboratively engaged in developing organizational strategies and solutions to such problems (Sebring & Bryk, 2000).

Leaders do this by nurturing human resources, and recognizing and aligning synergistic policies, structures, and supports that are mutually reinforcing and support the collaboratively developed and shared vision. Communities of practice work together to examine demographic, perceptual, achievement, and process or systems data (Bernhardt, 2004) and identify evidence-based interventions to address identified need areas (Wenger, 1998; Slavin & Fashola, 1998) and proceed to hold one another accountable for carrying out the vision (Elmore, 2004).

Beyond the internal workings of the school organization, effective leaders recognize and leverage opportunities for broader systems to support student learning. Specifically, the principal leverages systems external to the school organization, such as *district* goals, policies, and resources, to advance school goals. In addition, the master principal helps to shape district vision, goals, and policies by sharing best practices with district leaders and developing, identifying, and supporting policy opportunities to advance learning for all students across the district.

Outside of the organizational system, principals use resources from and work to advance *external communities,* helping members of these communities to recognize, share, and support the school's vision for student learning and broader community development. Members of these external communities include the following:

- *The local community*—embodied in the neighborhood, school cachement area, and the local community, including business and groups representing various community interests (Berg, Melaville, & Blank, 2006; Sebring & Bryk, 2000)

- *The professional community*—through membership and participation in professional associations and opportunities to learn from, and to document and share best practices with other educational professionals
- *The broader policy community*—which could include helping to shape and provide feedback on policy adoption and reauthorization and providing broader leadership across the state, nation, and internationally

The principal guides the organization to achieve its vision by developing and sustaining the organization and by developing, implementing, adapting, or undermining external policies and pressures in order to advance *student learning* and *organizational learning*.

SUMMARY

This chapter has introduced our model of leadership for *Learning First* derived from the experiences of leaders and successful schools that have made significant improvements in student learning and closed achievement gaps. It also draws from research on effective schools and school leadership to build a model of mastery in educational leadership.

Principals who practice socio-cognitive leadership, focus on the dimensions of leadership, and exercise levers of change can and do succeed in making quantum improvements in student learning in schools that are supportive, positive environments for teachers, staff, students, parents and community partners.

Figure 2.2 provides an outline of the remaining chapters of the book. In Chapters 3 and 4, we provide more explicit detail on the socio-cognitive leadership process, grounding it in the research and experience of schools that have successfully put learning first. We also provide tools based on these experiences to support school leaders in carrying out socio-cognitive leadership. Chapters 5 through 8 provide similar detail on how school leaders can focus school improvement efforts on the four critical dimensions of leadership. Chapter 9 describes in greater detail levers of change and provides examples of leaders who have used these levers to close achievement gaps and significantly advance learning for all students. We conclude with Chapter 10, which focuses on district-level leadership, recognizing that principals work within a larger system that supports and constrains their work.

Figure 2.2 *Learning First* Leadership

Socio-Cognitive Leadership	Dimensions of Leadership	Levers of Change
What	*Where*	*How*
• Shared vision • Problem setting with data • Evidence-based plan • Value-added results • Reflection for continuous improvement	• Advancing equity and excellence in student learning • Developing teacher capacity • Managing and aligning resources • Building an engaged community	• Individual leader • Organizational system • External community • District role
Chapters 3 and 4	Chapters 5, 6, 7, and 8	Chapters 9 and 10

Together, we believe these three elements constitute a model of leadership that provides a foundation for preparation, professional development, and recognition of master educational leaders. The work builds on a significant body of research on leadership for learning, as well as the voices and practices of master educational leaders who have successfully advanced student learning in their schools. What we view as particularly important about our model is the focus on leadership for learning as a social process of developing and utilizing communities of practice to problem solve and advance student learning. Furthermore, the model focuses on particular attention to value-added leadership—assessing schools as learning organizations by examining growth in student learning over time and comparing that to prior experience and comparison districts. It also has a strong and significant focus on advancing equity, which we believe is the most important and significant challenge for schools in the 21st century.

NOTES

1. The National Study of School Evaluation's work on effective leadership for school improvement provided an important foundation for the development of the socio-cognitive leadership model (NSSE, 2003). NSSE's work identifies vision, profile, plan, and results as elements of effective planning for educational improvement.

2. These categories were derived from the experiences of the master administrators we worked with, and are supported by the research literature. (See, for example, Darling-Hammond & Bransford, 2005.)

PART II

Socio-Cognitive Leadership

Setting Direction and Building Commitment

onsistent with other perspectives on leadership, the socio-cognitive framework views leadership as problem solving and builds on concepts of instructional and transformational leadership in educational organizations (Hallinger, 2003; Leithwood & Louis, 2004). Ken Leithwood (Leithwood & Louis, 2004) defines educational leadership as transformational, with a focus on problem solving that emphasizes *setting direction, supporting people,* and *creating organizational structures.* Phillip Hallinger (2003) defines educational leadership as instructional, with a focus on *defining the school's mission, managing the instructional program,* and *promoting a positive school-learning climate.* The socio-cognitive leadership model builds on the work of Leithwood, Hallinger, and others, emphasizing the leader's role in problem setting and problem solving in a community of practice. Specifically, the socio-cognitive model defines leadership from the perspective of

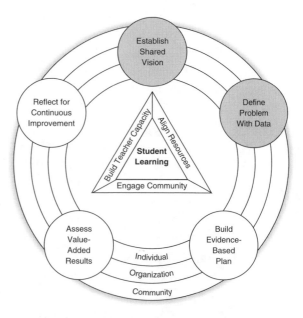

the individual leader supporting and developing a community of leaders engaged in *shared problem solving* using common cognitive decision-making strategies:

- Defining the vision or preferred state
- Problem setting with data
- Developing an evidence-based plan
- Assessing value-added results
- Reflecting for continuous improvement

The heart of socio-cognitive leadership is a shared cognitive structure that shapes thinking about problems. This cognitive approach to problem solving is widely shared by the school community. It is shared vertically from the superintendent to the classroom, impacting decisions at every level of the organization, and it is shared horizontally across organizational members, from teacher to teacher and from school to school.

In schools that put learning first, the socio-cognitive framework describes the way people think about problems. It shapes decision making by individual teachers regarding the design of curriculum for individual children and by school leaders and groups of teachers as they make decisions that impact schoolwide systems. It shapes decision making about instructional processes used by teachers and students, and by whole schools and school districts.

This chapter addresses the first two elements of socio-cognitive leadership—building a shared vision of the preferred state and collaborative problem setting using data. First, the vision provides an active, visible, and shared picture of a preferred state that motivates individual and collective action in the organization. An effective vision moves beyond broad platitudes (e.g., "All children can learn"). It articulates and specifies a clear target to strive for in advancing student learning. For example, "All third grade students will read at the proficient or advanced level as measured by the state achievement test by 2015." Motivation theory suggests that goals are most motivating when they are challenging but achievable (Locke & Latham, 1990; Vroom, 1995). Thus, the goal needs to be something that teachers can be equipped to achieve if an effective plan is put in place.

Next, the shared cognitive approach to problem solving begins with careful analysis of data. In combination, the vision and an understanding of the successes and gaps in achieving that vision as illuminated by data create energy and commitment to action. Data are used to make the work of public schools more public, to make the inequities in learning more apparent, more defined, and more solvable. In recent years, we have seen a significant shift in the way educators view data. In the past, data were viewed as part of the private student record describing individual student achievement and deficiencies in motivation and character. Today, high-performing schools use data to understand organizational effectiveness and identify deficiencies in systems and processes.

Everyone connected with these schools shares a common commitment to using data to define the problem so strategies can be identified to achieve the preferred state or vision. By committing to work together to achieve a shared vision and understanding the gaps in the current situation that need to be addressed to achieve that vision, socio-cognitive leadership gives teachers and others a sense of being a part of something important—something bigger than themselves—and fosters creative energy that fuels professional collaboration, collective problem solving, individual and group reflection, and a sustained commitment to action.

THE VISION OR PREFERRED STATE

In reviewing the leadership literature and research, perhaps the single most important and common theme that emerges is the importance of vision (Hallinger, 2003; Leithwood & Louis, 2004; Starratt, 1995). Similarly, in interviews with hundreds of teachers, students, parents, and school leaders, we have asked members of the school community to describe their school. As part of this description, we ask what the principal's vision for the school is and whether there is a shared vision among the school staff.

Universally, in the *Learning First* schools, the answer is crisp, clear, and consistent and focused on student learning. Teachers can talk about the collective vision shared by staff for the school, their own personal vision, and how these relate to a curricular vision that guides teaching practice in their classroom and throughout the school. They understand how their personal vision relates to the collective shared vision. They have internalized and committed themselves to the shared vision because it is consistent with their personal values. Pursuit of the vision provides a collective identity for the school and creates a safe space for collective problem solving. (Since we're all in this together, I'm not afraid to ask you questions that could help me contribute to the achievement of the vision. And since we're all in this together, I'm not afraid to offer suggestions, advice, and help to you to support achieving the vision.)

The extent to which vision frames action is perhaps clearest when talking to students and parents. Even young students can articulate the vision in high-performing schools using their own language and perspective. At Lincoln Elementary, the school's shared vision was to advance literacy through strengthening student writing skills. A third grader gave his experience of the vision as he complained, "This school is about writing. They make us write *all the time!*"

In less successful schools, teachers and school leaders struggle to articulate a shared vision. Their explanation of the shared vision is halting and inconsistent. Goals, values, teaching methods, and behavior management strategies vary from teacher to teacher, classroom to classroom. Staff members note that the school has a vision statement, but they can't quite remember what is in it. One principal was completely befuddled when we asked what her vision was for the school. Her actions suggested that she had a vision and was a committed leader, but her inability to articulate that vision and to keep it consistently visible to teachers created a leadership vacuum and a lost opportunity for teachers to work together around a common purpose. Ironically, the teachers in this school were very talented and committed to advancing student learning, but the vacuum created by a principal unable to articulate a vision or to challenge others to build a collaborative vision and pursue it together made teachers question their role in the school, and it made them wonder whether the principal really knew what she was doing.

As organizations, schools are cesspools of ambiguity. Teachers, parents, administrators, and staff observe and try to make meaning of actions that occur even though they have limited access to information to help clarify ambiguous events. A police car parked in front of the school, an irate parent, a decision to move a teacher from honors to remedial math, and other changes in the allocation of time, attention, or staffing provide opportunities for multiple interpretations by staff, parents, students, and community members. The principal can help the school community make meaning of actions that occur by consistently communicating a clear vision, by repeating stories that illustrate the vision in action, by creating opportunities to celebrate success in advancing the vision, and through the investment of resources to achieve the vision.

Leadership for learning means making decisions that put children first—sometimes the most politically powerless children. It cannot be successful and sustained in the face of a constant noisy buzz of second-guessing in the teachers lounge or in the halls on parent night. When this happens, the energy of the school focuses on critiquing leadership behavior and undermining tough decisions, and attention is drawn away from the real purpose of the school, advancing learning for *all* students.

In *Learning First* schools, ambiguity is minimized because teachers and others trust that decisions and behaviors are grounded in pursuit of the shared vision. Leaders who clearly and consistently articulate the vision help others interpret organizational action by using the vision as a lens to shape, define, and understand action.

What does it mean to have a *shared* vision, and what does it take to get there? A shared vision reflects a clear and strong focus on student learning as the chief priority for the school. The vision is grounded in a set of core beliefs about teaching and learning. The vision may be collaboratively developed with input from a broad spectrum of stakeholders, but it is consistent with core beliefs about advancing equity and excellence in student learning. It defines a compelling purpose and direction for the school and serves as a call to action for the school's stakeholders.

In *Preparing Teachers for a Changing World*, Darling-Hammond and Bransford (2005) identify a lack of curricular vision as a critical problem in low-performing schools and suggests that schools should hire teachers who have a well-developed understanding of their own vision of effective teaching and learning—a clear understanding of how people learn and what good curriculum should look like.

School leaders play an important role in addressing this lack of curricular vision. A first step in developing a shared vision is for the school leader to clarify his or her own core beliefs about how children learn, about what curricular approaches are effective, and to define a personal vision for his or her work in the school. A shared vision is built on a foundation of trust and open, honest communication. Principals need to be willing to lay their own closely held values and beliefs on the table if they are to engage in a conversation about values and beliefs with others.

Building a staff committed to a shared vision often involves more than just sharing and identifying common ground. It also involves taking a tough stand to ensure a schoolwide commitment to the vision. The leader can do this by supporting teachers who buy into the vision and maintaining high standards of accountability for all teachers to use the vision to guide action and to implement strategies identified to achieve that vision. Through this model of transparency, pressure, and support and by using hiring as a critical, strategic practice to bring in teachers who share the core beliefs underlying the vision, share the premise of the vision, and are committed to implementing the practices identified to achieve that vision, the teaching workforce will evolve over time toward an effective, committed community of practice.

The following case provides an illustration of how a new principal begins to build relationships, develop trust, and share expectations with staff as the foundation for the development of a shared vision of equity and excellence in learning for all students. Lowell Elementary School is a diverse urban elementary school that had a history of high performance but had undergone some recent challenges that weakened trust among members of the school community. The new principal sought to build trust and credibility with the staff and renew their commitment to advancing student learning.

Example: Lowell Elementary School

Below, Principal Lisa Kvistad reflects on her efforts to build a level of trust and open communication with her teachers as a foundation for building a shared vision for advancing student learning as she entered the principalship.

My transition to Lowell began in May, 2006. I still remember the day I walked into the auditorium to greet the 40 adults who would go on to ask me detailed questions about my beliefs about behavior, my feelings about poverty, and my responses to misbehavior. They asked me questions about multiage instruction, and they wanted to know how decisions were going to be made. Now, two years later, I still remind some of these adults about that first time we were together. Even over the past two years, it is still clearly evident that families and staff are invested in Lowell—they want to be proud of their neighborhood school, and they want to feel as if someone will listen to their concerns and respond with honesty and integrity.

That first summer, I made lots of coffee and spent lots of time talking with individual parents and groups of teachers. People told me their hopes and frustrations, and staff members responded honestly on the "Dreams and Challenges" sheet that I mailed to all folks who worked at Lowell. I knew that I needed to be myself—I needed to be very transparent and open. I didn't come to Lowell with all of the answers, but I did have some ideas to try as new systems and procedures took hold.

Along with building trusting relationships, I saw that it was all about the systems in the school that make it run smoothly. Not one staff member balked at system changes I proposed. Not one community member said, "It can't be done." Some people didn't like that the "Recovery Room" was gone (this was a space where students used to go and fix their problems with a staff member), but they understood that in its place came a renewed focus on individual interventions and ownership for more problem solving between teacher and student. We renewed our commitment to the "Above the Line" system of behavior management, and we met as a team over the summer to edit and revise this system significantly so that it would make sense to our school.

Even before the year started, I took a group of 15 staff members to the Ropes Course in the Madison Forest. We had a morning of problem solving together while we did activities that built trust and helped us to see each other in a new light. We all had lunch together afterwards at a local restaurant and truly enjoyed each other's company before the official school year began.

As a principal, I have always said that I need to love my job and adore the people I work with. I do—I enjoy the people I work with; we have fun, we work hard, we cry together, laugh together, and have tough conversations about many topics. I have always seen schools as human organizations—people are at different stages in their lives, and people need a variety of attention and support throughout the year. At the same time, educators need to be trusted to do their jobs and valued for their talents and expertise. This was a balance I really thought about my first year at Lowell, and I continue to be conscious of this all the time as I work with my staff.

Now that I am in my second year at Lowell, I feel a more collaborative culture. I see people laughing with each other, and I see teachers working very hard with children who have significant needs. We still have work to do, but I feel an environment of mutual respect that is tangible and focused. Our work isn't done—the initial transition years are just the beginning.

SOURCE: UW Madison Master Administrator Capstone Certificate Portfolio Document. Used with permission of Lisa Kvistad.

This example illustrates how Principal Kvistad developed foundational trust needed to engage in conversations with staff about their own personal visions in order to begin to build a collective vision together. Such conversations begin at the values level because it is the conscious connection to personal values that helps teachers internalize and embrace a shared vision for the school.

Many teachers may not feel that they have a personal vision for the school even though it is demonstrated on a daily basis in their beliefs and actions. The principal can advance the vision by helping teachers to realize that developing a personal vision and making that explicit is a part of the teachers' job as a professional. The principal can help teachers crystallize that vision by making it an explicit part of individual, small-group, and collective conversations. For example, the goal-setting process of evaluation for teachers could incorporate conversations that help to sharpen the teacher's curricular vision; department or grade-level meetings could include conversations about values, goals, and collective direction; and meetings with the broader school community could be used to confirm and reinforce the collective vision.

Beyond developing collective understanding, leaders that put learning first embody the vision in the stories, ceremonies, signs, behaviors, and structures that support teaching and learning in the school. The vision is not just a common set of beliefs or a mindless slogan, but it is embedded in the fabric of the organization, based on data and reflection, and provides a clear path that drives action.

The vision should be embraced by all, but it can initiate from multiple sources. In some schools, the district has developed a vision that provides common language, research and data foundations, professional support, clarification, and understanding. Individual schools interpret and embrace the district vision as it applies in their individual context. Chapter 10 discusses in further detail how the district can support socio-cognitive leadership in part through the establishment and implementation of a curricular vision. For example, in Madison, Wisconsin, the Madison Metropolitan School District's Balanced Literacy Framework provides clarity, common language, and definition to a districtwide curricular vision. In other schools, the vision is developed in the absence of such support or direction at the district level. Whether it emerges from district or school action, a common instructional framework is part of every successful school we have seen. (Although not a characteristic highlighted by Karin Chenoweth [2007], the case schools described in the book, *It's Being Done*, that made significant improvements in performance and closed achievement gaps all had a well-articulated, common instructional framework that facilitated shared problem solving for instructional improvement.)

Each school's vision is unique and should reflect the challenges, strengths, opportunities, and beliefs of the school community. But a description of vision doesn't seem complete without some discussion of what a shared vision might entail. From our work with successful schools, the visions that effectively drive instruction include the following:

- A conviction that the school is successful only when all children learn
- A constructivist view of teaching and learning, continuously refined by individual teachers and communities of practice
- A curricular vision grounded in social learning theory, an understanding of the use of the proximal zone of development, continuous progress, flexible grouping, differentiated instruction, and scaffolding to extend learning
- A theory of action that connects learning theory, research on effective classroom practice, the availability of tools and structural supports to advance teaching practice (such as instructional coaches), and curricular guides that embody the vision of how kids learn

- A clear and emergent picture of best practice—what a good school looks like, what a good classroom looks like, what good instruction looks like—even if this is not the current reality in the school

Within this broad framework, individuals may differ on their own specific vision of learning. *Learning First* schools vary in that some have a primary focus on improving test scores, while others take a broader view of learning that includes the social/emotional side as well as the intellectual side. Furthermore, the vision may be emergent, top-down, or adopted from an external source. An emergent vision is developed through collaborative conversations building on the knowledge, skills, values, and beliefs of the school community. A top-down vision may be initiated by the district or the principal, who shares their vision for the school and builds buy-in and support from staff. An external vision is one that is developed external to the district and adopted by the school. In one *Learning First* school, the principal and staff adopted the Accelerated Schools model, which has a clear and explicit vision for advancing student learning.

A vision built on the Bransford, Brown, and Cocking (1999) book, *How People Learn,* might include a clear vision of curriculum, a vision of an ideal community, and a vision of sound assessment practices. Regardless, engaging in conversations about personal beliefs in terms of a vision raises the level and importance of the discourse and reinforces a collective sense of direction and common purpose for the school community.

PROBLEM SETTING WITH DATA

Along with a clear shared vision that directs action, school leaders that close achievement gaps and put learning first work to establish a shared cognitive approach to decision making grounded in analysis of data to clearly define, or *set,* the problem (Halverson, 2004). The *data profile* helps to inform or sharpen the vision, and it also serves to clearly define gaps that exist between the vision and the current reality. With No Child Left Behind (NCLB), schools and school systems have become better at collecting, analyzing, and disaggregating data to identify gaps in student learning as measured by federal and state policy goals for progress on state tests.

Because the NCLB policy focuses on improving test scores among subgroups of students, educators are more aware of certain types of data, particularly, demographic data and state test scores. Due to the significant lag time between test administration and test results, many schools have also begun to administer formative assessments that are aligned with the state tests in order to provide more immediate feedback on student performance to inform ongoing adjustments in teaching and learning. Data retreats have become an important addition to a leader's repertoire because they provide an opportunity for a focused conversation on school data.

The challenge for leadership intent on closing achievement gaps and advancing learning for all students is to develop data profiling as a part of the socio-cognitive DNA of the organization. In other words, data analysis is not only part of an annual exercise or an occasional occurrence, but it is the way that members of the organization approach decision making for problems large and small. From a micro level, individual teachers make decisions about changes to instruction by gathering and analyzing data for individual students in their classrooms. At a school level, collaborative groups problem solve by considering the current data compared to the desired data suggested by the shared vision.

In this way, when data profiling is owned by the whole school community, it targets individual and organizational attention to a common set of problems. With a shared understanding of the organization, its strengths, and areas that need further attention to achieve the vision, data profiling reinforces and amplifies the vision and creates a stronger bond between members of the organization as they commit to overcoming the gaps to achieve that vision. This process also strengthens the imperative for collective problem solving, providing a foundation for the establishment of strong and effective communities of practice.

Research on communities of practice and professional learning communities suggests that the strongest communities of practice emerge from a common understanding of a problem, a desire to solve it, and a realization that by working together, we can make much more progress toward addressing the problem than if we worked alone. In turn, the opportunity to work together in a community of practice helps to advance individual and group learning, provides a sense of meaning for the work—which is very motivating—and gives individuals a sense of identity that is bound up in achieving the vision, further committing them to a meaningful role in community problem solving (DuFour & Eaker, 1998; Wenger, 1998).

Thus, by creating a comprehensive process for collecting, managing, and disaggregating data that is directly related to the vision and mission of the organization and incorporating this into all levels of the organization, the leader sets a tone and creates a common cognitive framework for how problems are addressed in this organization. The shared cognitive framework is developed and reinforced substantively and symbolically through consistent messages sent by leaders in the school as they solve problems together, as is shown by the following.

- Teacher evaluations, walk-throughs, and ongoing incidental and planned conversations about teaching and learning include a focus on data-based decisions.
- Professional development and data collection instruments show teachers how to collect and use data in everyday decision making.
- Staff meetings and meetings with other members of the school community include a repeated focus on the shared vision of the school and the data that illustrate where we are in achieving this vision.

Thus, socio-cognitive leaders create a shared vision and a common cognitive approach to decisions that includes analysis of data. Once this is established, structures that support professional community (common planning time, professional development, teacher walk-throughs) engage staff around a clear focus and direction and provide a common language and cognitive structure for identifying and addressing important problems.

The clear, shared vision enables an understanding of gaps between the current state and the preferred state, which galvanizes the organization to work together to address the vision gaps (Fritz, 1996; Lashway, 1997). Socio-cognitive leadership provides opportunities for the creation of a shared commitment to action, overcoming cultures of professional isolation.

What Kinds of Data?

Problem setting with data includes a comprehensive process for collecting, managing, and disaggregating data that is directly related to the vision and mission of the organization. The process includes analysis of data at all levels of the organization, from work with individual students, to groups of students, to classrooms, departments, grade levels, and schoolwide. Analysis of data includes the identification of trends, organizational strengths and weaknesses, projections, correlations, and emerging issues. It also includes comparisons to similar schools, benchmarking (comparison to best practice), and *value added* evaluation. The data are collaboratively reviewed to determine and revise and stimulate goals in the school improvement plan. Schools that succeed in putting learning first have sophisticated data collection, management, and analysis systems in place. They seek a variety of sources of data to inform their work.

Bernhardt (2004) identifies four primary types of data to inform decision making in schools:

1. Demographics: enrollment, attendance, drop-out rates, ethnicity, gender, grade level

2. Student Learning: standardized tests, norm/criterion-referenced tests, student work, teacher observations of abilities, authentic assessments

3. Perceptions: perceptions of the learning environment, values and beliefs, attitudes, observations

4. School Processes: description of school programs and processes

The data profile should include assessment of all four types of data. Educators have become fairly adept at analyzing demographic and student learning data (particularly standardized tests) and to some extent perceptual data (through climate and parent surveys) but are typically weaker at measuring and assessing school processes. Bernhardt (2004) notes that some of the more interesting analyses of data occur at the intersections between these types of data. For example, how well do African American males do in reading when they participate in a particular reading intervention, compared to those who do not participate?

To facilitate data analysis, we recommend a formal audit process in which the principal, leadership team, and/or staff systematically analyze data related to the dimensions of leadership. Throughout the book, we have included audit guides to illustrate the process of data analysis and the kinds of questions that can focus data gathering, analysis, and problem setting. These audit guides provide direction to school leaders regarding the kinds of questions to ask. The specific questions need to be tailored to the particular school context.

In most cases, data analysis fairly quickly identifies achievement and vision gaps as inequities in student learning and low expectations are brought to light. Sometimes these vision gaps reflect what Warren Bennis (Bennis, Goleman, & O'Toole, 2008) refers to as *vital lies*—the problems that we all know exist, but we tacitly agree not to talk about. These are like the unspoken truths that are covered up with lies that enable families to operate in the face of significant dysfunction, such as the ability to make excuses for the aberrant behavior of an abusive or alcoholic parent. In schools, vital lies are often used to explain away entrenched achievement gaps. In one diverse high school we worked in, for example, even the African American school leaders, staff, and parents explained away the consistent failure of African American students in the school as the students' fault—a problem of low student motivation. This vital lie enabled them to continue to maintain existing structures and approaches without having to question the foundations of a system that perpetuates inequality and discourages students whose experience tells them that being motivated is pointless.

The audit guides provide an opportunity to systematically review the data, surface vital lies, and unveil other problems with school processes and outcomes that need to be addressed in order to achieve the vision. The goal is to use data analysis as a tool to define and understand barriers to student success. Figure 3.1 describes the process we recommend be used to examine data to set the problem in the data profiling phase of socio-cognitive leadership.

Figure 3.1 Problem Setting With Data

Step 1: Understand the Baseline

Examine demographic patterns, recent historical trends, and expected future trends in the data (e.g., student body makeup, teacher demographics, knowledge and experience, community partnerships and collaborations).

Step 2: Examine Disaggregated Outcomes

Disaggregate student outcomes by groups identified in Step 1 to highlight achievement gaps and strengths. Continue this analysis until you have a clear understanding of the gap between your vision or preferred state (e.g., *all* students learning to high levels) and the current reality (the vision gap).

Step 3: Analyze Current Practices

Examine current practices, programs, and participation that lead to the outcomes identified in Step 2. Consider strong programs or processes that support excellence and programs or processes that contribute to vision gaps.

Step 4: Consider Common Problems

In addition to examining current practices, consider common problems that contribute to weak educational outcomes or the absence of evidence-based practices known to address the specific achievement gaps identified in your school.

Step 5: Answer Summary Questions

Use the guiding or summary questions associated with each dimension of leadership for learning (advancing equity and excellence in student learning, developing teacher capacity, managing and aligning resources, and building an engaged community) as you build the evidence-based plan described in Chapter 4.

The data profile should build an understanding of the current school context as it relates to the vision. Specifically, it should focus on student learning as measured by a variety of measures of student learning—not just test scores. The data profile should be conducted with an eye toward creating an understanding through data of how to continue to advance learning in the school. Furthermore, data systems should be nested and should include information about the individual child, the classroom, the department/grade level, and the school, including comparative data to understand the school benchmarked against similar schools, best practices, and districtwide and statewide performance.

Chapters 5, 6, 7, and 8 provide audit tools to facilitate the collection and analysis of data related to advancing equity and excellence in student learning, developing teacher capacity, managing and allocating resources, and building and engaging internal and external community.

Data-Driven Instructional Systems

Richard Halverson (Halverson, Grigg, Prichett, & Thomas, 2005; Halverson & Thomas, 2007) has developed a model that describes how schools use student-learning data to inform instructional and curricular decision making. The Data-Driven Instructional Systems (DDIS) framework describes the structures and practices school leaders use to support data-driven organizational and instructional decisions. Specifically, the framework suggests that data profiling occurs through a series of identifiable structures and processes. Two of these processes include the following:

1. *Data Acquisition*, which includes *data collection, data storage,* and *data reporting*

2. *Data Reflection*, which includes *data retreats* and *local data reflection activities*

Other aspects of the DDIS framework relate to the other phases of socio-cognitive leadership, so we focus here on these two elements of the framework. Data collection identifies the types of data to be examined. While test scores are an obvious component of a data-driven instructional system, data collection can include a variety of sources of information, including things like student grades, demographic and observational data on teachers and teaching practice, student placement and behavioral patterns and processes, community survey data, budget information, master schedule and curricular information and processes, technological capacity, and curricular information.

Another element of data acquisition focuses on data storage and retrieval capabilities. Halverson notes that data are stored in various locations, and retrieving relevant data in a timely manner sometimes involves overcoming logistical and political barriers to accessing and using various types of data. For example, districts may collect student test score data, but the data may not be accessible at the classroom level due to barriers erected by school cultures or unions concerned that their members may be held accountable for student learning gains even when they have limited control over curricular materials, student assignment and motivation, student mobility, and student preparation coming into their classrooms.

Data analysis often relies on available data, although the pressure to access timely and relevant data on student learning has led many districts to seek products from testing companies and other vendors to provide more relevant and timely information to assess student learning needs.

Data reflection focuses on collaboratively reviewing and evaluating available data at the whole school, grade level, or teacher team level. Halverson notes, "Successful data reflection involves problem framing and concludes with the determination of goals for a plan of action" (Halverson et al., 2005, p. 8). Data retreats provide an opportunity to gather together and analyze data, identify gaps and prioritize areas in need of improvement, develop hypotheses that might be further investigated to get at the sources of areas in need of improvement, and begin to develop goals that build toward the establishment of a plan to address problem areas in the data (DuFour, Eaker, & DuFour, 2008).

These analyses of data provide focus and attention to areas in need of improvement to advance learning for all students. Among the schools we have worked with, a number of schools have implemented the data tracking wall concept in which individual student's names are posted in a teacher-controlled room to show how many and which students have achieved proficiency (typically in reading) and to follow the progress of students as they move up toward proficiency as the year progresses (McKinley, Puma, & Witherow, 2006). At most schools, the markers for students are color coded and clearly identifiable by classroom. Teachers' initial concerns about being identified as having a large number of students who are not succeeding are typically replaced over time by a shared commitment and competitive spirit for the school as a whole to succeed in moving all children forward in their learning.

SETTING THE PROBLEM: THE LEARNING FUNNEL

By collaboratively developing a shared vision and shared understanding of the data profile for the school as a whole, socio-cognitive leaders provide broad direction for the school and move teachers and other stakeholders to achieve the shared vision or preferred state. In successful schools, this occurs through an iterative process. A broad vision is set. Data are analyzed to identify barriers to achieving that vision. The data analysis informs the establishment of a more focused vision. Data are analyzed further to better pinpoint that more narrow and focused vision. The process of goal setting and data analysis continues down to the specific changes that need to be made at the level of the individual child because it is at the level of the engaged student that learning occurs, and the entire system advances.

Borrowing from Conrad and Serlin (2006), in Figure 3.2, we depict this analytic process as a learning funnel. At the top of the funnel is the school context. A vision is set to provide broad direction for the school, and data are profiled to understand this broad context. Moving down the funnel, the members of the school community use data analysis to identify gaps in achieving the vision and set a more focused direction for moving student learning forward. With this sharper vision, data are analyzed to understand gaps in achieving that vision. This occurs on multiple levels from the whole school to the interaction between the teacher and the individual child and across the four dimensions of leadership for learning:

Figure 3.2   The Learning Funnel: Setting the Problem

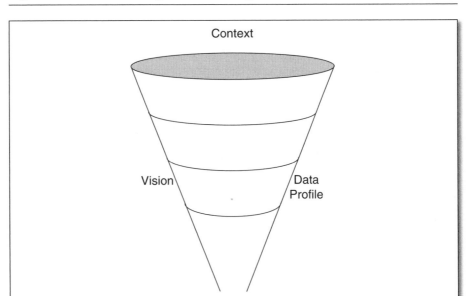

Advancing Equity and Excellence in Student Learning, Developing Teacher Capacity, Managing and Aligning Resources, and Building an Engaged Community.

The vision and the data analysis are grounded in the school's particular context, but each successively focused effort to improve teaching and learning reflects the broader vision, data profile, and context, and is embedded in it. Thus, socio-cognitive leadership involves not just setting one vision, but it involves a series of goal-setting exercises within each of the dimensions of leadership for learning to achieve the broader vision of equity and excellence in student learning. The vision at the top of the funnel may be set by the school board, the district, the school leader, or the school community. Moving down into the funnel, vision setting may become more local so that at the bottom of the funnel, problem setting may occur at the level of the teacher establishing a vision and examining data with an individual child to move their learning forward.

For example, the school's context describes the demographic, organizational process, student achievement, and perceptual reality of the school. With this broad context as a foundation, the school community establishes a vision of moving 90% of the students to proficiency on the third-grade reading test. Analysis of data shows that boys and students with special needs achieve at lower levels than other students. A vision is set to strengthen and lengthen reading instruction and student engagement in reading targeted for these groups. Analysis of data suggests specific reading needs common throughout the group, and specific goals are set by the third-grade team to address these needs. Within the classroom, teachers establish a vision for individualized, small-group, and whole-group reading instruction that is linked to the broader school vision, and teachers work specifically with struggling students to ensure each child's learning needs are being met. Thus, the broader vision of advancing learning for all students is addressed through increasingly focused and narrower visions and data analysis until the learning goals are set, understood, and addressed for each individual child.

Because Vision Setting and Data Analysis are part of the intellectual DNA of the *Learning First* organization—from the whole school to the individual classroom—a consistent and aligned process occurs in which members of the school community understand the broader vision and context, and they work in their field of influence to envision a more specific preferred state aligned with the broader vision, informed by data analysis to better understand and set the problem.

In Chapter 4, we turn to the remaining steps in the cognitive model, developing an evidence-based plan, assessing value-added results, and reflecting for continuous improvement.

DATA RESOURCES

Measures of Academic Progress (MAP), http://www.nwea.org/

Assessment for Learning and Teaching (ASPIRE), http://www.ascd.org/programs.aspx

Evidence-Based Plan, Value-Added Results, and Reflection for Continuous Improvement

The previous chapter focused on the first two phases of socio-cognitive leadership: establishing a shared vision and developing a shared understanding of the progress and barriers to achieving that vision through the analysis of data. In the vision-profile phase of socio-cognitive leadership, the goal is to define critical problems that need to be addressed in order to close achievement gaps and advance learning for all students.

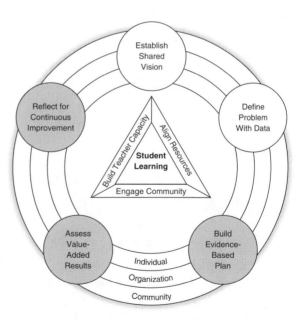

Defining or setting the problem based on a clear, shared vision and collaborative analysis of data may seem like an obvious approach to problem solving, but unfortunately, in education as in many other fields, solutions are often identified because they are considered innovative, they have worked somewhere else, or because some members of the school community find them to be compelling. We refer to this as the Fire, Ready, Aim approach to educational leadership. In many schools, administrators and teachers don't solve problems, they adopt solutions.

In the education system of the 20th century (and in many schools today), teachers taught the curriculum, and students learned or they didn't. Administrators offered solutions, and they worked or they didn't. But 21st-century schools can't afford these random acts of administration. We made the case in Chapter 1 that changes in demographics and global economic competition reflected in accountability policy mean that schools are accountable for student learning. Teachers are responsible for ensuring that they implement teaching strategies grounded in data to ensure that students learn, and administrators are responsible for administering solutions that address problems identified through careful analysis of data in order to address gaps in organizational efficiency and student learning.

Thus, we spent a considerable amount of time in Chapter 3 describing the learning funnel: how schools identify specific problems that are grounded in the vision and analysis of data. In this chapter, we move to the next phases of socio-cognitive leadership: *developing and implementing an evidence-based plan, assessing value-added results,* and *reflecting and making adjustments* to support continuous growth and improvement.

We present these ideas in a separate chapter to provide sufficient opportunity for depth of focus, but we emphasize the importance of the connection between problem setting and problem solving. Schools that close achievement gaps and significantly advance learning for all students do not practice random acts of administration. Instead, they adopt plans that are targeted to address problems identified through the problem-setting process.

EVIDENCE-BASED PLAN

The *plan* phase involves identifying and implementing an evidence-based plan to address problems defined through the analysis of data. Plans address the dimensions of leadership to advance student learning (see Chapters 5–8), and their focus varies considerably depending on the local context, history, strengths of the faculty and students, and gaps in achieving the vision.

However, *Learning First* leaders share some common principles in their approach to identifying and implementing effective plans:

- The community of practice works together to define goals and objectives for the plan to advance the vision of student learning. These goals are shared, clearly specified, measurable, and challenging enough to require the school to stretch to achieve them, yet they are attainable within a reasonable timeframe.
- The strategies and comprehensive action steps chosen to address the goals come from evidence-based principles of high-performing systems with similar profiles and are directly aligned with the school vision and identified problems.
- Key leaders' responsibilities are clearly identified and include ways to mobilize others' talents.
- Resources are fully dedicated to the improvement strategies and additional resources are secured.
- A systematic and comprehensive assessment plan for evaluating and documenting baseline measures, growth, and the process of implementation is in place.

Developing an Effective Plan

Principals that lead schools to advance equity and excellence in student learning rely on leaders distributed across their school, district, and community to help identify potential elements of the plan (Spillane, 2006). Plans take advantage of opportunity (building on grant-funding opportunities; seizing unifying events; combining efforts with teacher, school, community, or district strengths and initiatives; utilizing school improvement planning cycles; harnessing the energy and enthusiasm of committed personnel) but maintain fidelity to addressing vision gaps and advancing the vision.

The school as a community engages in consideration and development of the plan so that its strengths and intended purposes are widely understood by school stakeholders. Plans may emerge from ideas generated within the learning community or from outside sources, such as research findings, professional associations, media attention to particular innovative practices, teachers with previous experience with a similar intervention, or other networks.

The principal balances the need to allow for teacher leadership with the importance of making a real and symbolic visible personal commitment to the plan. This could occur through principal participation in an exploratory professional development session along with key teacher leaders, participation in site visits to similar schools that have implemented the proposed plan, ongoing consultation and listening sessions with teachers about the plan, participation in development of the plan, information gathering to support evaluation of the intervention for its applicability to the school, and/or investigation and acquisition of potential resources to fund implementation.

Throughout our work with schools that have made quantum leaps in student learning, we saw no examples of schools that implemented their teaching and learning interventions without some form of additional external financial support for their efforts. The external support came from a variety of sources—district, community, foundation, government—but they all had some form of support in addition to reallocation of the regular school budget to support the teaching and learning reform. These resources were used to provide professional development, travel, coaching, planning time, community building, troubleshooting, and modifications to the physical plant to support teaching, learning, and student engagement. The importance of resources to the success of the teaching and learning interventions is not clear. It is possible that additional resources are necessary for schools to make quantum gains in student learning. But it seems equally plausible that the resources were not a cause of learning gains but an effect of a dynamic, successful school organization. The resources may have been an outgrowth and reflection of the commitment and focus of the schools to advance student learning, often in challenged, diverse school settings. The schools sought and were able to draw in additional resources to support their work because of their strong and clear moral commitment to advancing the learning of struggling students and because funders recognized the capable leadership of a community of practice committed to student learning. In this sense, the resources may reflect the presence of Jim Collins' *flywheel* effect, serving to accelerate and support an organization that has already put significant effort into putting the flywheel in motion (Collins, 2001).

In most cases, the interventions were adapted from reforms that had been successfully undertaken in other similar schools, but they were customized to address local needs and conditions. Reforms were often piloted a particular grade level or within a subset of the school, and the school retained a commitment to evaluating and refining the reform to strengthen it, and make it work. However, we also saw examples of leaders who realized that a particular effort was not working, and abandoned it when needed to move on to a more effective intervention. Leaders that put learning first never settle for less than the achievement of the shared vision, and they approach implementation with a commitment to vision and an analytic mindset.

The plan includes identification of baseline data to enable assessment of progress toward the goals and efforts to identify formative assessment data that will provide guidance through implementation for refinement of the plan. A typical approach to educational leadership might be to evaluate the success of a plan by its implementation. But leaders that close achievement gaps and significantly improve learning for all students evaluate success by its effect on *student learning.* Thus, assessment of growth in key indicators provides feedback about the effectiveness of the reform.

The following example provides an illustration of the ways in which evidence-based plans address problems identified through vision setting and data analysis. In the example, West High School identified a vision gap, searched for alternatives to address the gap, found a workable plan in place in another school district, visited the school to get first-hand information about its effectiveness, and leveraged grant funds to support implementation of the plan.

Example: West High School

As with many large high schools, lunchtime triggered a number of student behaviors that disrupted learning at West High School. West, a diverse urban high school with about 2,100 students, including approximately 40% minority and low-income students, has a long history of academic success, reflected in the 29 National Merit scholars it boasted in 2005. With a highly educated and highly skilled teaching force, West operates more like a university campus than a typical high school. But West, like many urban high schools, faced persistent achievement and engagement gaps between minority and white students.

Over the past three years, the principal of West, Ed Holmes, worked with staff to develop a vision of equity and excellence in student learning. An analysis of demographic, process, perceptual, and achievement data suggested that the design of the lunch period was a significant problem.

Through the 2005–2006 school year, West had a rotating two-and-a-half-hour lunch period, which ran from 11 a.m. to 1:30 p.m. During that time, lunch drove nearly everything in the school. It tied up the administrative team and security staff for half of the school day. Students would often skip their midday classes so they could eat with friends who had been assigned to a different lunch schedule, so midday course attendance was consistently low. In addition, transportation and employment barriers created an engagement gap as many minority and low-income students could not stay after school to participate in club activities or obtain extra help from teachers.

On the recommendation of a teacher leader, Principal Holmes visited a Maryland school that had addressed similar problems by instituting a single 50-minute lunch period. He came back intrigued by the idea. The challenge was how to ensure that all students would have a seat for lunch if they chose to stay on campus. Mr. Holmes used grant funds to renovate and furnish a second gym that had been used to house equipment and provide practice space for a gymnastics team of only eight to 10 students.

The new lunch period was named Lunch and Learn to reflect the learning club, enrichment, and academic support activities that occur during the hour-long lunch

(Continued)

(Continued)

period. Lunch and Learn is a highly successful structural reform that has helped to better engage students and teachers alike in student learning.

In order to avoid having 2,100 students hit the cafeteria simultaneously, West instituted a mandatory 20-minute advisory period for all freshmen at the beginning of the lunch period, facilitated by seniors selected from a broad spectrum of students for their leadership abilities. During the advisory period, freshmen receive guidance in ways to have a successful high school experience. The advisors take a course that provides lesson plans and training to support their teaching of the 20-minute sessions and cover a broad array of academic and social issues.

West operates in an urban environment with strong union and contract restrictions. Teachers by contract have a 30-minute lunch period, so the one-hour lunch provides them with a longer break from classes, and they are asked to find ways to support the school during the other half hour. To date, nearly 80% of staff is actively engaged in supervision at lunch, including tutoring, club advising, and other academic enrichment activities. The administrative staff maintains a wall chart posted near the cafeteria that denotes times, meeting places, and staffing of lunch-hour activities. The current wall chart list includes 110 different activities, including clubs reflecting a broad spectrum of student and staff interests, tutoring, test makeup, teacher team meetings, and various support groups. Many of these activities take place for the entire lunch hour, and students bring their lunch to the meetings.

In addition, the gym remains open for students who want to play basketball, and students who want to leave campus to eat at local eating establishments are able to make it back to class on time. The school has sufficient seating for 1,500 students in the two cafeterias.

Despite fears from staff and community members that the hour-long lunch might provide greater opportunity for trouble, the Lunch and Learn program has greatly reduced absenteeism and conflict during the lunch hour. One lunch has also freed administrative staff time and reduced costs for cafeteria workers and security, increased student and faculty engagement in learning, enhanced teacher relationships with students and school climate, and supported student learning by expanding opportunities for contact between teachers and students.

In West's case, the vision was to maintain excellence in student learning while working to close achievement gaps. The data suggested that student engagement and attendance around the lunch period contributed to the gap. The principal identified a plan for beginning to address the student engagement and attendance problem and did a site visit to a school that had addressed this problem through Lunch and Learn. The school implemented the plan and has closely tracked data on student engagement and attendance to assess its effectiveness. They have used climate surveys, teacher and student perceptual data, student engagement and achievement data, and school behavior and attendance data to assess the effectiveness of the intervention. While the intervention has not unilaterally succeeded in closing the achievement gap, it has addressed the lunch-hour absenteeism problem, freed up administrative staff for other work, increased teacher engagement in student learning and student engagement, and created a safer and more positive school climate.

SOURCE: UW Madison Master Administrator Capstone Certificate Portfolio Document and Site Visit. Used with permission of Ed Holmes.

ASSESSMENT OF RESULTS

The next phase of socio-cognitive leadership is assessment of results. In this phase, there is a clear, shared understanding of the desired results for student learning, which are directly aligned with the school's beliefs, mission, and vision. Each member of the faculty, staff, and administration can describe how the desired results for student learning are related to the school's vision. A comprehensive data collection process is used to establish baseline data in critical areas of student learning and to assess changes in learning that result from the intervention (see Figure 4.1).

Figure 4.1   Value-Added Leadership

A Basic Method for Measuring Value-Added Leadership

1. Measure key outcomes before and after implementation of the plan.

2. Assess outcomes for individuals participating in the plan compared to those not participating or compared to growth rates prior to plan implementation for the same or a similar group.

3. Compare gains to expected growth to assess progress and refine elements of the plan as appropriate.

Examples of Outcome Measures

Student Outcomes

Learning: State Test Scores, Formative Assessments, Reading Levels, Common Assessments, Learning Compared to Grade Level Standards, Student Enrollment and Success in Higher Level Courses, Equity Audit Data (Figure 5.2)

Attendance and Participation: Attendance Records, Homework Completions, Participation in Extracurricular Activities such as Clubs, Activities, Music, and Sports Programs

Behavior: Behavioral Referrals, Suspensions, Expulsions

Classroom Outcomes

Teaching Practice: Changes to Curriculum and Instructional Practices, Student Movement Between Flexible Groups, Walk-Throughs, Teacher Self-Assessment, Teacher Capacity Audit Data (Figure 6.3)

Grade Level/Department Outcomes

Learning: Qualitative Measures of Academic Press/Achievement Culture

Teacher Team Problem Solving/Collaboration: Teacher Responses to Community Assessment Tool (Figure 6.4)

(Continued)

Figure 4.1 (Continued)

School Outcomes

Learning: State Test Scores

Engagement: High School Survey of Student Engagement (HSSSE), Local Surveys, Socio-Cognitive Leadership Site Visit (Resource B) or Leader Self-Assessment (Resource A)

Resources: Financial, Human, and Physical Resource Audit Data (Figures 7.2, 7.4, and 7.5)

Community Outcomes

Parent Participation: Attendance at Parent Teacher Conferences, Volunteer Activities, Learning Nights/Open Houses, Surveys or other Measures of Parent Support for Student Learning

Community Support: Participation in Community Outreach Activities, including Participation, Financial Support, Volunteers; Partnerships, Community Audit Data (Figure 8.2)

Value-added assessment is used by stakeholders to improve teaching and learning. In value-added assessment, baseline data are compared with data after the implementation of the new structure, curriculum, process, or plan. This can be as simple as calculating a gain score or as sophisticated as comparing student results with forecasts of expected student performance given student demographics, performance history, attendance, and programming. At the school level, there is rarely capacity to do this more sophisticated modeling, but some assessments provide guidance about expected growth curves, and a growing number of school districts, such as the Dallas Independent School District and the Milwaukee Public Schools, have developed the capacity to calculate value-added growth expectations for schools, classrooms, and individual students (see http://varc.wceruw.org/).

Data analysis is used to provide formative feedback to revisit and amend the plan to ensure its effectiveness in terms of improvements in student learning. The analysis of student learning includes a variety of assessment and evaluation measures beyond required state tests.

The thorough value-added analysis of student learning needs based on assessment results is conducted collaboratively by stakeholders. Stakeholders also conduct surveys and analyze stakeholder perspectives on the strengths and limitations of student learning and priorities for improvement.

Study teams comprised of stakeholders also review the latest educational findings, future trends, "user inspired research," and school reform models that have implications for defining desired results. Value-added results may also be measured in terms of improvements in processes and perceptions. However, improvements in processes and perceptions should be viewed as a means to the end of improvements in teaching and learning and not ends in themselves.

Assessment of results needs to occur in a timely manner. Research on the implementation of value-added assessment systems in Milwaukee and Chicago by the Wisconsin Value Added Research Center (VARC) suggest that results need to be assessed with very quick turnaround in order to provide meaningful information to inform instructional design decisions and address learning gaps in real time. The immediacy of analysis of results requires that teachers, schools, and districts "design data collection and data warehouse systems so that the right kind of data is collected at the right time, analyzed almost instantaneously, and then immediately fed back to school and district staff" (VARC, 2008).

Thus, data collection and analysis plans should be established early in the planning phase and may build on data analyzed in the data-profiling phase. It is critical that data sources be identified and planned for early in the process and that the types of data analyzed include sources that can be gathered and analyzed in real time.

REFLECTION FOR CONTINUOUS IMPROVEMENT

Reflection is a critical phase because it is through reflection, revisioning, and retooling that teaching and learning is continually refined and enhanced and moves student learning forward. Reflection involves consideration of the entire socio-cognitive leadership process, including the role of the shared vision, problem setting with data, evidence-based plan, and value-added results to inform and sharpen future action.

Organizational Learning

Research on organizational learning identifies several mistakes that can be made in the reflection stage that impede accurate learning from experience. These include *superstitious learning*, which involves attributing student achievement or other results to the implementation of the plan when the results were actually produced by an external event or some other unknown cause. This could occur if some external event (a fire across the street during the state test) interrupted student concentration and artificially lowered test scores, and the data analysis failed to recognize the event and interpreted the outcome as caused by the intervention.

Another problem that could occur is the effect of *competency traps*, in which teachers become really good at a particular teaching approach and switching to a new, more effective approach results in a temporary implementation dip in learning outcomes as teachers struggle to master the new approach. Long-term it may be superior, but there may be great reluctance to invest in learning the new method. The reluctance to overcome the competency trap will be reinforced in teachers' minds because of the likely drop in performance before teachers are able to master the new approach and realize the benefits from it.

Competency traps make it hard to try new approaches because everyone is so good at using the older, less effective technology. The classic example of this is the design of the typewriter keyboard. New designs have been developed for many years that enable trained typists to produce at much higher levels. But because the current keyboard is universal and everyone who types is familiar with that keyboard, there are huge barriers to moving to the new, more efficiently designed keyboard (March, 1988).

Learning may also be role constrained, in which structural barriers impede changes in individual behavior to effectively implement the plan. For example, if teachers don't have enough time in their day to carry out their duties and redesign curriculum to address identified learning needs, they may not fully implement the plan. Thus, it is critical that the assessment of results includes attention to both process and product—How well was the plan implemented? What were the barriers to implementation and implementation successes? and What were the results? If the plan was not fully implemented, it may be necessary to invest additional time and effort on implementation before abandoning the plan as ineffective.

Reflective Practice

Another approach to reflection is to consider research on reflective practice. Lee Schulman and Donald Schön are both known for their work to advance the concept of reflective practice in education. In a recent article, Schulman (2000) notes three things that go awry when individual learning doesn't go well: amnesia (forgetting what you've learned), fantasia (not understanding that you misunderstand), and inertia (not acting on what you've learned). Successful reflection involves a careful and objective look at the facts—not just test scores but also the context, data on process, demographics, and perceptual data—to understand current practice and its effects.

Like all schools, *Learning First* schools face political barriers to improvement grounded in feelings of ownership of particular types of favorite practice. But these schools overcome the politics by establishing a vision that is a compelling call to action shared by all members of the school community. Thus, teachers and others are able to understand the data and are willing to adjust to changes in practice and work to make interventions effective. This is sometimes difficult because stakeholders may be committed to current practice because of prior investment in it or simply because they enjoy it and have felt successful doing it in the past. Changes to the unknown can be disconcerting and require willingness to take risks.

Schulman (2000) quotes David Ausubel, a cognitive scientist who wrote, "The most important single factor influencing learning is what the learner already knows. Ascertain this and teach him accordingly" (p. 39). School leaders need to understand what teachers already know and work with them to overcome biases and misconceptions to move toward practice that advances learning for all students.

THEORIES OF ACTION AND SINGLE- AND DOUBLE-LOOP LEARNING

A useful approach to reflection—and to the development of the plan to begin with—is to consider the theory of action underlying the plan. The theory of action explains beliefs about the relationships between the underlying mechanism by which the plan will address the vision gap. For example, heterogeneous grouping is an effective strategy for closing achievement gaps because it provides rich learning opportunities by establishing common high expectations and exposure to complex material for all students. It allows high achieving students to model engagement, motivation, commitment, study skills, and results. As teachers are challenged to provide complex material to challenge high achievers, they must also grapple with learning styles and build foundational knowledge for all students to succeed to high levels.

Being explicit about the theory of action fosters a richer examination of the ways in which the plan is being carried out. For example, if students are placed in heterogeneous classrooms but teachers do not establish high expectations, strong students will not be challenged, and weaker students will not benefit from the heterogeneous grouping. Building shared understanding of the theory of action and attending to implementation of the plan to achieve desired results enables richer reflection on the results of plan implementation and refinement of the implementation of the plan to strengthen its effectiveness.

In this way, analysis of results and reflection provide opportunities for more careful examination of the conditions required for the theory of action to hold. Where the conditions have not been met, this would direct leadership attention and action to strengthen those conditions and provide an opportunity for the theory of action to hold.

If the required conditions are met, but the expected results are not achieved, it could call into question the underlying theory of action and lead to consideration of other approaches (or new theories) to explain how to achieve the desired results. Reconsideration of underlying theories of action is referred to as double-loop learning (Argyris & Schön, 1978). In single-loop learning, reflection leads to minor adjustments in response to analysis of results. In double-loop learning, it leads to reconsideration of the fundamental premises or theories of action that shape the reform, leading to more significant changes in approach to addressing the teaching and learning challenge.

A final important aspect of socio-cognitive leadership is helping people make sense of the work—finding ways to talk about the work and to celebrate the efforts of those who have invested in it, while continuing to move the organization forward.

Thus, the reflective process should include opportunities for celebration of successes, periodic examination of data to consider the validity of the underlying premises of the reform, identification of specific steps that can be taken to strengthen the reform, and consideration of the effectiveness of the reform as a whole with a particular emphasis on student-learning considerations. The process may also take into account political, social, cultural, and financial considerations in moving forward.

The reflective process should be firmly grounded in a systems perspective by considering integration and connections among improvement efforts and a strong desire for continuous improvement for the organization and the individual. It should include a focus and consideration of the four dimensions of leadership—advancing equity and excellence in student learning, developing teacher capacity, managing and aligning resources, and engaging community—and their actual and potential future role in advancing the learning initiative. It should also consider ways to strengthen and better utilize communities of practice in advancing student learning through the initiative.

PART III

The Dimensions of Leadership for Learning

*T*he dimensions of leadership for learning define *where* leaders focus attention in order to close achievement gaps and advance learning for all students. The dimensions of leadership include four critical areas of focus for educational leadership to improve student learning. The first is the core outcome dimension, and the others are process dimensions that support the sharp focus on advancing student learning. The dimensions include the following:

1. *Advancing Equity and Excellence in Student Learning* by closing achievement gaps and advancing learning for all students (Chapter 5).

2. *Developing Teacher Capacity* by advancing the abilities of all teachers, including teachers who struggle (Chapter 6).

3. *Managing and Aligning Resources* by acquiring and deploying the organization's financial, physical, and human resources to advance student learning (Chapter 7).

4. *Engaging Community* by developing and involving internal and external communities to advance student learning (Chapter 8).

Chapters 5 through 8 define each of the four dimensions of leadership for learning, and show how school leaders can apply the socio-cognitive leadership framework to each of the four dimensions to foster communities of practice that close achievement gaps and advance learning for all students. For each dimension, we suggest how leaders collaboratively develop a shared vision of a preferred state and collect data related to that dimension to identify, define, or set the problem. We draw from common evidence-based strategies to address problems related to that dimension and discuss strategies for assessing improvements in key outcomes related to the plans. Finally, we provide case examples and discuss ways to foster and encourage reflection to advance effective leadership for learning within each dimension.

Advancing Equity and Excellence in Student Learning

The first dimension of leadership for learning provides the critical focus for leaders who put learning first. Inequities exist in every school. Common gaps in opportunity and performance that occur include systematic differences among subgroups of students in achievement, attendance, discipline, access to the most challenging curricula, and participation in extracurricular activities. Furthermore, there are students in every school who are not being challenged. Schools that advance equity and

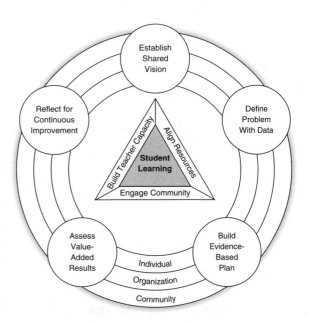

excellence work to design curricular structures that differentiate curriculum and offer meaningful challenges to students at every level.

Thus, advancing equity and excellence in student learning means closing achievement and opportunity gaps and advancing learning for all students. Educational leaders do this by focusing the socio-cognitive leadership process on accelerating learning for students who struggle and students who are not challenged and by continually expanding access to high quality teaching and learning for all students.

Figure 5.1 shows how the socio-cognitive leadership model is applied to problems of advancing equity and excellence in student learning.

Figure 5.1   Advancing Equity and Excellence in Student Learning Through Socio-Cognitive Leadership

1. Begin with a clear, shared vision of the preferred state: What will equity and excellence in student learning look like in the curricular and social context of this school?

2. Collaboratively examine data to assess equity and excellence in student learning: What achievement gaps exist? What pockets of excellence exist in the school?

3. Develop evidence-based plans on how to address the vision gaps: What programs, curricula, and pedagogies address vision gaps to advance equity and excellence in student learning?

4. Examine student learning and student engagement outcomes: How have targeted student-learning outcomes improved as a result of the plan?

5. Consider areas for further improvement and build on successful strategies: How can we refine our strategy to continue to advance equity and excellence in student learning outcomes?

ESTABLISH THE SHARED VISION OR PREFERRED STATE

Schools that succeed in narrowing or closing achievement gaps do so by raising the achievement of *all* students. The process begins with the establishment of a clear shared vision of high levels of learning for all students. In Kennewick, Washington, a *Learning First* district that has dramatically raised the performance of students throughout the district, this occurred through a negotiated agreement that the school district would strive for 90% of its students to achieve proficiency on the state assessment.

Similarly, with the vision "Where All Reach Excellence" in 2007, 100% of the fifth-grade African American students at diverse Keith L. Ware Elementary School in Fort Riley, Kansas, scored at the exceeds-standards (9%) or exemplary level (91%) compared to a state average of only 32% of students in these categories (19% at the exceeds-standards level, 13% at the exemplary level). Moving students to the proficient level was insufficient for Ware. Even as they met the goal of all students at the exceeds-standards level, they continued the push to strive for a goal of exemplary performance for all students.

When all students are challenged, closing the achievement gap means moving many more traditionally low-performing students into advanced content and classes and challenging all students at the highest levels. The specific achievement goal becomes a clear target and a focus of staff, student, and parent energy and effort. A key role of school or district leadership is to be a strong anchor and steward for this vision, motivating, supporting, and maintaining focus on the goal for teachers, students, parents, and the public and accepting nothing less than achievement of the goal as a clear sign of success. Personal and institutional success or failure is measured by progress toward the goal, and the entire enterprise is committed to continuous improvement to reach and exceed the goals set by the vision.

Unfortunately, in many schools and districts, leadership touts the school's successes and downplays, explains away (with vital lies), or ignores the embarrassing details—the areas that the school is less successful in. Many high schools, for example, wave the flag of success in the form of National Merit scholars, award recognition, and star alumni while burying statistics about the academic failures of low-income, minority, or limited English–proficient students. In schools that put learning first, a commitment to pursuit of the shared goal and belief in the ability of the school to achieve that goal enables school leaders and staff to face what Jim Collins (2001) refers to as the *brutal facts.* With all of the data on the table, leaders can work with the community to set high goals, bringing failures to light and attention so they can be addressed.

DEFINE THE PROBLEM WITH DATA

The quest to address inequities in student learning begins with *understanding the baseline*—disaggregating available data by race, family income, gender, track, special education status, and student mobility.

Next, the principal and school community need to understand critical relationships between the disaggregated data and student-learning outcomes. To address the inequities, the analysis must move from *examining disaggregated outcomes* to *analyzing current practices,* examining questions such as the following:

- What barriers has the school created to accessing challenging classes?
- How does the discipline policy impact student access to classroom instruction, and how can it be refined to maximize learning opportunities for all students?
- What specific areas of the subject are students excelling in, and what areas are they struggling with?
- How can we work to strengthen teaching practice to accelerate learning for all students? For struggling students?
- What supports have been provided to help students learn the material, and how could they be strengthened?
- How has the school approached developing parent support for student learning? What expectations do we have of parents, and how can we better help parents help their children succeed?

For each of these questions, additional perceptual, process, and student achievement data are needed to define the problem, in order to meaningfully address it. The process of defining relevant data, gathering, and analyzing it will vary from context to context depending on the focus and scope of the problem and the range of data resources already available through classroom, school, or district assessment processes.

A good place to begin to develop effective, regular, and systematic data to analyze and advance student learning is with the data that are already available. What are the sources of data that the school, district, or state already collects, and what can be gleaned from these data sources? Schools that close achievement gaps and significantly improve learning outcomes for all students find ways to use available data to provide meaningful input into instructional decision making.

If additional data are needed, the data should

- Be readily accessible and timely
- Provide specific direction to inform instructional decisions
- Provide information on the learning needs of individual students
- Be widely shared, understood, and reviewed on an ongoing basis

Lackland City Elementary School in San Antonio, Texas, is a high poverty, largely Hispanic, PreK–5 school that has as its goal that 90% of students will be successful on the Texas Assessment of Knowledge and Skills (TAKS). Despite its high poverty and limited English speaking population, the school has exceeded its goal with 90% to 100% proficiency on all measures on the state test. Lackland's story is described more fully at the end of this chapter. Here, we focus on their use of data to identify areas for focused improvement. First, the school uses assessment as an integral part of their strategy to determine student learning needs and advance mastery learning. Key assessments include the following:

- Daily assessments of student progress obtained by teachers walking around the classroom during the lesson and daily assessments at the end of the lesson that ask students to solve one problem that captures the essence of the lesson so teachers can get a clear indication of each student's level of understanding and learning needs to inform the next day's lesson
- Weekly quizzes on concept development
- Unit tests that assess students' ability to remember and apply knowledge
- Eight-week assessments in reading to enable the school to adjust student reading levels based on recent progress
- District curricular benchmarks tests to assess student understanding of key standards
- District promotion standards tests to assess student mastery of knowledge required for promotion to the next level
- The state assessment: TAKS

Table 5.1 shows how these and other data are assessed to inform instruction and ensure that student learning needs are continually understood and addressed.

Table 5.1   Lackland City Elementary Levels of Data Analysis

Who Analyzes the Data?	What Is the Focus of the Data Analysis?
Classroom teacher	Compare individual students
Instructional content facilitator	Compare individual students and teachers
Principal	Compare classes and grade levels
District	Compare individual students, classes, and schools
State	Compare individual students, classes, schools, districts, and subgroups

Using ongoing data analysis at all levels of the organization, Lackland is able to maintain a strong foothold of understanding of student learning progress and needs and can adjust and focus curriculum and instruction to continuously move students forward. Lackland City Elementary has developed a strong history of success with its high poverty, English Language Learner (ELL) population. Despite its recent success, Lackland was not always a high achieving, diverse school. Initially, a foundational analysis was needed to better understand the school, its strengths and challenges, and critical gaps that needed to be addressed to advance equity and excellence in student learning and move the school forward.

Figure 5.2 provides guidance for such analysis, identifying the types of data that anchor or set the problem in a clear understanding of the barriers that exist to achieving equity and excellence in student learning. It

Figure 5.2   Audit Guide: Advancing Equity and Excellence in Student Learning

---

Step 1: Understand the Baseline

What is the distribution of students, recent historical trends, and expected future trends by the following?

- Race and Cultural Background
- Poverty (Free and Reduced-Price Lunch Eligibility)
- English Language Learners
- Students With Identified Special Learning Needs
- Student Mobility
- Community Context

Step 2: Examine Disaggregated Outcomes

Search student learning data for patterns in achievement to identify strengths, inform the vision, and direct school improvement efforts. Compare overall achievement to state averages, schools with similar demographics, or other comparison groups. Disaggregate data by race, poverty, classroom, grade level, special education status, student mobility, or other factors indicated by your analysis in Step 1. Continue this analysis until you have a clear understanding of the gap between your vision of the preferred state (*all* students learning to high levels) and the current reality (the vision gap).

For all schools, consider the following:

- Indicators of student learning, such as test scores and learning outcomes
- Attendance
- Grades and promotion rates

For middle and high schools, also consider the following:

- Credit accumulation toward graduation by year
- Students fulfilling college entrance requirements
- ACT/SAT/AP results
- Post school outcomes

Step 3: Analyze Current Practices

Examine student access and participation in current programming that may support or impede student-learning outcomes. What is the participation of students by race, poverty, grade level, special education status, student mobility, or other factors that could contribute to the vision gaps identified in Step 2? Consider who participates in various activities and then examine school processes underlying student access or assignment to programming. What does student participation look like for the following?

- Behavioral referrals/disciplinary actions (suspensions, expulsions, etc.)
- Success in gatekeeper courses
- Supplemental academic programming, such as extracurricular activities, summer school, tutoring, after-school programs, gifted and talented, and so on
- Courses by level of course (special education, basic, regular, advanced)
- Enrichment programming, such as music, art, sports, foreign languages, and so on
- Strong and meaningful relationships with adults in the school

What underlying processes affect student access to effective learning opportunities?

- Class size
- Student assignment to experienced teachers
- Behavior management practices and policies
- Assignment processes for special education
- Structure of special education programming
- Formative assessment
- Support for curriculum and instruction development
- Ability to move between tracks or trajectories
- Other processes specific to your local school context

Step 4: Consider Common Problems

In advancing equity and excellence in student learning, the following may need to be addressed:

- Are students in advanced placement or advanced content courses representative of the entire student body?
- What intentional or unintentional barriers exist to gifted and talented, advanced placement, or enrichment programming?
- Are all but the most severely disabled students placed and supported in regular education settings?
- Is high quality coteaching occurring between special and regular education teachers in all regular courses with special education students?
- Does grouping for services result in de facto segregation of students by ability level or background?
- Does teaching practice address each individual child's learning needs?
- Is there a culture of formative assessment that informs instruction to ensure that each child's learning is appropriately scaffolded and supported?
- What supports are in place to ensure that a child with a history of failure can achieve at the highest levels?
- How does the school identify and fuel each child's passion for learning?

Step 5: Answer Summary Questions

- How will you work to help students who struggle?
- How will you work to help students who are not challenged?
- How will you improve access to high quality teaching and learning for all students?

includes both process and outcome data to help identify potential inequities or lack of press in learning opportunities for students.

We refer to Figure 5.2 as an audit *guide* because the specific questions that you ask will be dependent on your school context. The goal is not to exhaust the school community in the data analysis phase but rather to use data analysis as a critical tool to define and understand barriers to student success.

First, systematic data are examined related to student demographics, including the makeup of the school in terms of race, gender, grade level, family income (free and reduced-price lunch participation), ELL, and special education assignments by category. These demographic categories raise attention to family background and student learning needs and can provide a foundation for Step 2, disaggregating student learning data to better understand inequities in access to learning opportunities and outcomes that need to be addressed. Outcome data should be disaggregated for all students by critical demographic and placement categories. These data will indicate how students are doing in comparison to other students, similar schools, the district, state averages, and benchmarks. Schools that close achievement gaps and significantly advance learning for all students track student outcome data over time and use all available information at hand to help understand and interpret student-learning outcomes.

In data collection and analysis, Step 3 examines current practices in student programming and placement that contribute to school successes and vision gaps. These data provide information about the types of instructional supports currently available to students to scaffold and advance learning. They also provide information about the barriers to advanced learning opportunities. Which students are named in behavioral referrals and disciplinary actions? Which students are targeted for remediation services? Which students are involved in gifted and talented, Advanced Placement, or extracurricular programming? These data raise issues related to learning opportunities. For example, what is the representation of African American males in gifted programming or Advanced Placement courses?

Once patterns of potential disparate impact are identified, Step 4 involves taking a closer look at these educational processes and their potential impact on student learning. This analysis raises questions about the policies, processes, and programming that might be the focus for school improvement efforts to strengthen learning opportunities for all students and identifies common problems that we have seen in schools as they struggle to advance equity and excellence in student learning. For example, in some high schools, Advanced

Placement class sizes are very small, while lower-level core courses have higher enrollments. This practice invests resources heavily in high performing students and disinvests in lower performing students. An examination of class sizes across student demographic and academic groups can therefore illuminate potential opportunities to reallocate resources toward the students most likely to benefit from smaller class sizes.

Similarly, an examination of disciplinary and remediation policies might show that students are routinely removed from instructional settings in order to be disciplined or receive supplemental instruction (e.g., in reading). We have visited a number of elementary schools where misbehaving students sit for hours in the office either awaiting attention from the principal or in order to prevent further disruptions of the regular classroom. In *Learning First* schools, behavioral modifications are designed to emphasize positive reinforcement for good behavior and minimize the amount of time that disruptive students are out of the classroom. Thus, these students maintain an ongoing connection to the curricular content, which improves their ability to participate in class activities and learn the material. An examination of discipline and behavioral policies might suggest ways in which behavioral policies might be restructured to minimize disruption to instructional settings while maximizing learning opportunities for all students.

Another critical area for focused examination is the instructional processes related to education for special needs students. Low-income minority student populations are often over-identified for special education services. Furthermore, despite legal requirements that students be placed in the least restrictive environment and research that supports inclusive education, many special education students are educated in pull-out programs that limit student access to challenging curriculum. A careful examination of student outcome data in concert with the settings and instructional methods by which special education students receive instruction can provide critical information about the ability of current placement strategies to promote strong learning outcomes for students with special needs.

Finally, consider assessment practices, utility and timeliness of assessment data, and current practices regarding the ways individual teachers and learning teams review assessment data and work together to problem solve and modify strategies to advance student learning.

It is important not only to recognize, understand, and celebrate successes but also to identify areas for further improvement and focus. For example, one school we worked with had made significant progress in moving students from a novice to proficient category on the state assessment.

Yet very few students were achieving at the exemplary level. By working with the school to examine their data, we were able to help them recognize their significant success in improving student learning and also to set new goals for advancing learning for students to the highest levels.

The audit analysis enables leadership teams to identify critical gaps in educational processes and outcomes for focus. Using these data, the school can identify multiple problem areas that need to be addressed in order to advance equity and excellence in student learning. With the problem *set*, the school can move forward to begin to identify strategies for improving teaching and learning to address critical learning gaps.

BUILD AN EVIDENCE-BASED PLAN

Figure 5.3 provides some examples of common evidence-based strategies to advance equity and excellence in student learning. These strategies are present in the schools we have seen that have succeeded in closing achievement gaps and advancing learning for all students. The strategies were adopted and designed to address specific problems identified through

Figure 5.3   Common Evidence-Based Interventions to Advance Equity and Excellence in Student Learning

---

Socio-Cognitive Leadership

- Shared Vision of High-Level Learning for All Students
- Equity Audit: Collaborative Data Analysis and Planning
- Research-Based or Evidence-Based Instructional Materials and Methods
- Value-Added Assessment of Results
- Reflection and a Commitment to Continuous Improvement

Inclusive Instructional Environments

Positive and Consistent Behavior Management

- Above the Line, Below the Line, and Bottom Line
- Line Basics
- Positive Behavior Interventions and Supports (PBIS)

Individualized Instruction and Mastery Learning

- Diagnostic Assessments (MAP)
- Common Assessments
- Differentiated Instruction
- Flexible Grouping (whole-class instruction followed by heterogeneous and/or homogeneous small-group work)

- Individualized Education Plans for Every Student
- Teaching and Reteaching

Teacher Growth and Public Practice

- Common Planning Time
- Observation of Peer/Mentor Teachers
- Team Teaching
- Walk-Throughs
- Teachers Observing Other Teachers
- Co-Teaching
- Instructional Coaching
- Professional Development that Is Continuous and Embedded

Matching Learning Environment to Student Learning Needs

- Staff Strength Assessments
- Student Assignment Grounded in Teacher Strength Assessment and Student Need Assessment Data
- More Time: Afterschool Tutoring, Saturday School, Summer School, Year-Round School
- Outside Community Resources: Tutors, Mentors, Volunteers, Partners, Universities, Outside Scrutiny
- Extracurricular activities and sports used to build academic culture for learning

analysis of data, and they represent a common set of strategies that *Learning First* schools have implemented to advance learning for all students. While we do not provide a comprehensive review of research associated with the strategies, there is a strong evidence base to support their effectiveness in addressing student learning needs.

Socio-Cognitive Leadership

First, schools that put learning first use socio-cognitive leadership: They maintain a strong, clear, shared vision of learning for all students and an unwavering commitment to advancing equity and excellence in student learning. They use data to identify learning problems, including effective use of diagnostic assessments to provide immediate feedback to teachers to address student learning needs. They also share a set of instructional strategies that enable them to achieve the vision and address vision gaps.

Inclusive Instructional Environments

Learning First schools have inclusive instructional environments in which students with disabilities learn with other students in the regular classroom (Frattura & Capper, 2007). The instruction in these inclusive classrooms involves highly collaborative team teaching. On one of our site visits, we witnessed an inclusive classroom with a regular and special education teacher working together. The teachers took turns leading the lesson. Following whole-group instruction, the class was divided into working groups according to current student understanding and performance in the subject. After one teacher finished working with a small group of students with special needs, we asked her how long she had been a special education teacher. Surprised, she replied, "Oh no, I am the regular education teacher." The two teachers provide a powerful example of how regular and special education teachers can work together as a seamless instructional team whose goal is to address the needs of *all* students.

Despite research evidence that suggests that inclusive instructional environments provide the most effective context for addressing the learning needs of all students (Staub & Peck, 1995; Weiner, 2003), many schools continue to use less effective instructional arrangements for special needs students. These include one of two common arrangements, neither of which typically challenges special education students to achieve to their potential: (1) isolating students in a separate classroom or (2) grouping students in the regular classroom without a special education teacher, with a special education teacher disengaged from the lesson, or with a special education teacher who provides limited support of the special education students with limited interaction with the regular education teacher. These strategies are problematic. The first poses a risk that the students in the separate special education classroom will not be exposed to the same level of curricular content and that the academic press of the classroom will be reduced to accommodate the lowest achieving students in the class. The second approach fails to fully utilize resources available to the learning environment. Furthermore, without being fully engaged in the content, pedagogy, and instructional goals of the regular education teacher, the special education teacher fails to take full advantage of teaching and learning opportunities.

When regular and special education teachers are cross-trained, they can work together as a productive, collaborative team to advance instructional strategies that better address the needs of all learners. The training in differentiated instruction and flexible grouping that special education teachers receive provides an important pedagogical foundation for scaffolding learning for all students. Similarly, the regular education teachers have important content knowledge to challenge all learners. The more that special and regular education teachers work together as a close-knit team, the more they draw on one another's strengths to advance learning for all students.

Positive and Consistent Behavioral Management

Another important strategy for advancing learning for all students is the design of behavior management systems and referral processes. Effective behavior management is critical because disruptive students impede learning for themselves and for others, reducing the efficacy of the learning environment for everyone. In addition, students who are removed from the classroom due to disruptive behaviors (sometimes for hours or days at a time) are missing important instructional opportunities. These students are put at risk educationally because of instructional time lost when they are out of the classroom.

Therefore, schools that put learning first set clear and consistent behavioral expectations for students and design behavioral interventions to minimize barriers to learning. They coach students on appropriate behaviors and use motivational tools to encourage positive student behavior. These processes encourage and model positive behavior while minimizing time spent away from the learning environment for students who disrupt the classroom or otherwise break school rules. *Learning First* schools use behavioral management plans that are implemented consistently across teachers, contexts, and grade levels. The plans are designed to clearly teach and reinforce positive behavioral expectations rather than waiting to punish students for dangerous or disruptive behavior. They include regular opportunities for analysis and reflection on how the school can be restructured to support positive student behavior.

Research on developing an effective schoolwide behavior management system identifies the following characteristics, which are consistent with the systems we found in *Learning First* schools: "(1) total staff commitment to managing behavior; (2) clearly defined and communicated expectations and rules; (3) consequences and clearly stated procedures for correcting rule-breaking behaviors; (4) an instructional component for teaching students self-control and/or social skill strategies; and (5) a support plan to address the needs of students with chronic challenging behaviors" (Fitzsimmons, 1998).

A variety of positive behavior management systems exist, and many schools design their own plans. A key element of effective plans is continuous analysis of outcomes and refinement of the plan to address unique features of the specific school context. One plan we have found that looks very promising is the Positive Behavior Interventions and Supports (PBIS) System, which has been adopted by the State of Illinois as well as a number of other schools and districts nationwide.

The plan builds on the concept of Response to Intervention (RTI) and focuses on providing integrated academic and behavioral interventions that proactively address learning and behavioral management issues in the least restrictive setting. For most students, academic and behavioral expectations and interventions are taught in the regular classroom setting and focus on proactive, preventive systems that reward appropriate behavior and have a continuum of consequences for inappropriate behaviors.

For 5% to 15% of the students, secondary interventions focus on small-group-targeted rapid-response interventions to reinforce positive behavioral and academic expectations. A small percentage of students (1%–5%) require individual interventions, which are assessment-based and high intensity and focus on helping students avoid problem contexts and reinforce positive behaviors. Together, RTI and the PBIS focus on helping students to be fully functioning by providing clear expectations, rewards, and interventions to support positive behavioral outcomes (see http://www.pbis.org/ for examples).

PBIS clearly establishes behavioral expectations, teaches students appropriate behavior in context, and provides individualized student plans for early intervention when students fail to achieve academic and behavioral targets (Sprick, 2009). The Madison Metropolitan School District adopted PBIS in its middle schools in 2007 and in the first year experienced as much as a 70% drop in behavioral referrals in some schools. Early evidence suggests that this type of early academic and behavioral intervention, along with clearly communicated expectations that are embedded in the curriculum, is an extremely effective approach to student behavior management.

Another promising behavior management model that focuses on clearly defining and reinforcing behavioral expectations is the Corwin Kronenberg Above the Line Classroom management system, which has been adopted by a number of districts. The following case is an example of a school that adopted Kronenberg's model along with a broader systemic approach to supporting positive student behaviors.

Example: Mendota Elementary School

Mendota Elementary School is a diverse, urban elementary school. Ten years ago, the principal, Sandy Gunderson, came to Mendota—a school, at the time, known throughout the district as a challenged institution. Principal Gunderson worked with community organizations to revitalize both the school and community. The school has become a safe, positive, high-achieving learning environment. Along the way, Principal Gunderson and her staff analyzed behavioral referrals and discovered that there were a large number of referrals, disparately impacting African American boys. They created a data log to record behavioral referrals to better understand who was being referred, under what circumstances, and with what results. The analysis identified three circumstances that resulted in high levels of behavioral referrals: the playground before school, hallways during transitions, and classrooms for specific groups of students.

To create consistent expectations for positive behavior, the school implemented the district's schoolwide behavior management plan, Kronenberg's Above the Line, Below the Line, and Bottom Line behavior management system, which defines behaviors that are positive and reinforced (Above the Line), negative or disruptive (Below the Line), or particularly disturbing and dangerous (Bottom Line). In addition, teachers established rules to reinforce polite and considerate behavior (e.g., taking your hat off in school, putting your coat on the bench next to you instead of on the lunchroom table, addressing others politely).

To address the playground altercations identified in the data analysis—which were often complicated because teachers on playground duty did not know the children involved in the altercation—children were asked to line up by grade level, each grade at a different door around the school. Thus, grade-level teachers, who had a relationship with the students in their line, could stand outside and talk with the children until it was time to come in. Students were expected to stand in their grade-level line until they were allowed to come in for the morning breakfast program. The breakfast program provided an important transition time to allow the children to settle down to the rules, behaviors, and routines of the school. Teachers talked to students as they came into the cafeteria, and escorted students to their classrooms after breakfast.

To address hallway disturbances, children were taught line basics—a behavior management approach in which students are asked to face forward, stand behind the person in front of them, keep eyes open, hands and feet to oneself, and walk quietly on the right side of the hallway. In addition, school entrances were rearranged so students had less distance to walk to get to their classrooms. Related to hallway transitions, teachers noticed that they wasted a lot of instructional time during the day moving children from classroom to classroom during transitions. The teachers made it a contest between classes to see who could conduct the quickest and quietest transitions, and students got very excited about lining up in 15 seconds or less to compete with other classes for the best transition.

Finally, behavior management referral processes were changed so that the adult responsible for intervening in disruptive classroom behavior would go to the classroom to calm the child down rather than sending the child down to the office. That way, students learned that acting out did not earn them a free pass out of the lesson, and they had to learn to manage their behavior within the classroom context. These structural changes supported students in reducing misbehavior and dramatically reducing loss of instructional time caused by behavioral issues.

SOURCE: UW Madison Master Administrator Capstone Certificate Portfolio Document. Used with permission of Sandy Gunderson.

Mendota Elementary provides a good example of the kinds of positive behavior management approaches we saw in *Learning First* schools. Common approaches used in these schools include the following:

- Line basics
- Relationship building
- Teaching polite, respectful behavior and clearly establishing behavioral norms and expectations
- Systemwide positive behavior management plans such as Corwin Kronenberg's Above the Line/Below the Line behavior management system
- Teacher responsibility for student misbehavior to limit student removal from the instructional environment
- Involvement and support of parents in behavior management, including building shared expectations and language for behavior management, and teachers contacting parents to report both positive and negative student behaviors (see www.pbis.org for more information)

Individualized Instruction/Mastery Learning

Schools that close achievement gaps and advance learning for all students continuously assess student learning through diagnostic assessments such as the Northwest Educational Association Measures of Academic Progress, or MAP test. MAP is a strong resource because it is aligned with state accountability tests and provides specific and immediate feedback to teachers on student learning. It is a computerized adaptive assessment, which means that as students answer questions correctly, the questions get more difficult, and as they answer questions incorrectly, the test adjusts to easier questions to more quickly and accurately pinpoint student performance levels. Use of the MAP test has spread rapidly; across the country, more than 3,400 districts use MAP testing for diagnostic assessment (see http://www.nwea.org/ for more information).

Armed with information about student learning needs, schools that significantly improve student learning use whole-group instruction followed by homogeneous or heterogeneous small-group work to take students from their current understanding and move them forward. Grouping is flexible but designed around current learning needs. Student learning is frequently assessed, and students are regrouped to continuously challenge and address learning needs for all children. Teachers use teaching and reteaching strategies and develop individualized education plans for every child to continuously move learning forward.

As needed, schools provide additional learning opportunities to support student learning. At Wright Middle School, the school partners with the local recreation department to provide after-school tutoring. Teachers assign homework in specific subjects on the days in which tutors in those subjects are available in the after-school program. This strategy has enabled students whose parents have limited English speaking abilities or limited time or opportunity to help their children with homework to have the help they need to successfully complete homework assignments.

Teacher Growth and Public Practice

Another critical strategy for closing achievement gaps and advancing learning for all students is focusing on building professional learning communities and feedback systems to support teacher development by making teaching practice public and providing teachers with support to strengthen teaching practice, such as through the use of instructional coaches. In virtually every case, *Learning First* schools have used some form of an instructional coaching strategy. The socio-cognitive leadership model is framed on the idea that all learning is social, and indeed, these schools have strong communities of practice in place in which teachers work together to advance teaching practice through collaborative problem solving, observation of other teachers, feedback from administrators and other teachers using walk-throughs, and experience working together with other teachers in team-teaching situations. All of these practices strengthen teacher capacity by creating new experiences and social networks to develop and extend teaching knowledge and skills.

Match Learning Environment to Student Learning Needs

Advancing equity and excellence in student learning requires careful attention to how students are matched with teachers to ensure that every student has an opportunity to access expert teachers in the school. These schools have a clear understanding of teacher strengths, and they allocate teacher resources to maximize learning opportunities for students. They also partner with external agencies and find additional time for student instruction to ensure that students who take a little longer to learn challenging material have the support they need to be successful.

Challenges Specific to High Schools

High schools represent a particularly unique set of challenges to advancing equity and excellence in student learning through socio-cognitive leadership that merits some focused attention. High schools are larger, more bureaucratic, departmental, and operate with more of a disciplinary culture. Thus, they provide a more challenging environment for creating a collaboratively developed and widely shared vision, providing opportunities for meaningful collaboration among staff, and overcoming structural barriers to learning than the smaller, more informal culture of an elementary school. In addition, the older and more independent student population creates challenging barriers to student learning due to issues related to student engagement and motivation. Figure 5.4 provides

Figure 5.4   Overcoming Barriers to Learning at the High School Level

- What does the school do to support students for whom the current environment is not working? (e.g., How does the school address truancy, failure to turn in assignments, or dropouts?)
- What scaffolding (e.g., structured learning support, including modified teaching methods; more instructional time during or after school or on weekends; tutoring support) does the school provide to help students succeed in regular and advanced courses? Is this support optional or required?
- What opportunities exist for students to develop personal relationships with adults? Where do those occur? What structures support them? What barriers are there to such access?
- Are behavioral expectations common, transparent, communicated clearly to students, and consistently reinforced?
- What are the gateway courses to higher level coursework, and what does it take to get into and succeed in them? Do they intentionally or inadvertently limit access to higher level courses, or do they foster student success and engagement so that more students can enter advanced or accelerated courses? Who decides, and on what grounds?
- How does the school ensure that all students are challenged? How does the school push middle-performing students to the next level? What are the opportunities and barriers to move from regular to advanced work? In practice, how many students move fluidly from one level to the next?
- What curricular or extracurricular offerings are correlated with student attendance, academic success, and engagement? What curricular or extracurricular offerings or placements are correlated with poor attendance, academic failure, and dropping out?

a list of questions that high school leaders might ask to illuminate critical barriers to progress at the high school level, including a focus on gateway courses, student-teacher relationships, student engagement in learning, parental relationships, and behavioral expectations of students.

Answers to these questions can provide important data to set the problem of student engagement and learning at the high school level. A vital lie or hidden secret about high schools is that millions of kids fail. High school cultures often encourage curve grading as failing students is thought to reflect high standards. But many, many students drop out of high school because they fail so many classes that they are unable to make up the credits needed to graduate. High schools that put learning first find ways to address the learning needs of all students. They set standards of performance and support students to achieve those standards so they can pass the course and move to the next level. Interventions occur early, and students are required to receive extra time and extra help to master required content.

ASSESS VALUE-ADDED RESULTS AND REFLECT FOR CONTINUOUS IMPROVEMENT

A commitment to leadership for learning requires a willingness to assess progress of new initiatives. The data analysis phase provides important data to set the problem. This phase provides important data to assess progress toward the goal and refine or retool the intervention strategies to make them more effective.

Typically, accountability data focus on student test scores, and indeed, we recommend that key learning outcomes be assessed through the regular assessments used to measure school and student progress. In addition, other types of data (perceptual and process data) may be collected to assess the extent to which teachers, staff, students, parents, or community members are aware of shifts in attitudes, behaviors, expectations, or practices. It is important in designing the intervention to consider what kinds of accountability data will be needed to measure success or failure so that baseline data can be collected that enable a value-added assessment of progress given the reform strategy. Accountability data, like data in the problem-setting phase, need to be collaboratively analyzed, shared, and widely understood. They begin to help the school reset their strategy and consider ways to refine what they have been doing to continue to advance student learning outcomes.

In the next section, we provide more detail about the case of Lackland City Elementary School, which provides an example of a school that embodies the focus on advancing equity and excellence in student learning through the socio-cognitive leadership lens.

Example: Lackland City Elementary School

After six years as principal of a well-appointed, high performing, high socio-economic status elementary school, Jerry Allen called his superintendent and asked if he could change schools. The superintendent was surprised because Principal Allen already worked at the best school in the district. But Mr. Allen wanted a challenge. He wanted to make a difference. So he asked to be appointed to the most struggling school in the district.

The superintendent complied, and Mr. Allen was transferred to Lackland City Elementary, a school on the Mexico border with 98% economically disadvantaged students. Today, Lackland Elementary is an exemplary school, a designation that means that 90% of Lackland's students perform at a proficient level or above on the TAKS.

Teachers at Lackland are very committed to achieving the goal. Two years ago, when, after much hard work to attain 90% proficiency in science, the students missed the 90% mark by one point, the teachers cried. Last year, continued concentrated effort brought student science scores over the 90% mark, enabling the school to be identified as an exemplary school according to Texas standards. The teachers have great pride in achieving this designation but realize that the effort needs to be sustained to retain the exemplary designation status.

To get there, Lackland has developed a goal that at least 90% of its students will achieve at a proficient level on the state test. Even with high mobility, high rates of economic disadvantage (95%), and high numbers of limited English proficiency (20%), Lackland has achieved its goal and sustained the exemplary designation.

How do they do it? First, they have a vision that is a very clear, focused goal. The principal serves as a steward for the vision, and teachers define their success or failure by whether they have achieved the goal. Teachers are very committed to the goal, and school action is driven by whether this step will bring them to the 90% goal. Sophisticated data analysis is conducted at the classroom, campus, and district level. At LCE, the teachers teach a little, test a little, teach a little, test a little. . . . Assessments occur as follows:

- Daily, as teachers walk around the room and note students who understand and fail to understand the lesson; some teachers collect an exit card at the end of each lesson, which is an index card with one problem to quickly assess how well students understood the day's lesson. By quickly flipping through the cards, the teacher can see which students understood the lesson and which students need additional support to get it.

- Weekly quizzes assess concept development.
- Unit tests assess student's ability to remember and apply the concepts.
- Eight-week assessments are conducted in reading, and student reading levels are adjusted accordingly for the next eight-week unit.
- District curriculum benchmark tests assess students' progress in mastering content according to state standards.
- District promotion standards tests assess students' ability to master content required for promotion to the next grade level.
- State assessment tests are given in March, April, and in the summer to provide summative assessment of student, school, and district progress.

Teachers work together to examine assessment data, and the school adopts *research-based intervention strategies* to advance student learning. The staff is reluctant to endorse a particular strategy, instead noting that there are multiple research-based strategies that schools could choose from. They recommend that other schools select a strategy that works for them—one that is well developed and has an evidence base to suggest that it is successful in helping students learn, in their case to the 90% goal.

Curriculum is aligned horizontally and vertically, with grade-level lesson plans guiding instruction for all teachers at a single grade level. Reading occurs in a 90-minute block each day, and students are flexibly grouped across grade levels according to reading ability. The school provides opportunities for teaching and reteaching within and outside the regular curriculum. For example, LCE runs an afterschool instructional program to provide additional support for student learning. Teachers provide tutors with information about student learning and current curriculum so the afterschool program can address specific student learning needs and supplement current unit instruction.

Using Title I funds, the school has hired full-time curriculum facilitators in math, reading, and writing. The facilitators purchase and distribute curricular materials and train teachers to use them, provide training to teachers new to the school, serve as substitutes so teachers can observe other teachers' classrooms at the same grade level, co-teach and coach teaching, lead team meetings once a month in the subject area, and provide other supports as needed to address learning gaps identified through ongoing disaggregation of data.

Because curriculum is aligned by grade level, the curriculum facilitators can work with teachers by grade level to provide materials and professional development to support upcoming instructional units. Teachers are expected to know the state and district curriculum content goals and standards, plan for and teach the required skills, follow a timeline for testing, ensure that all skills are covered, and align curriculum vertically to prepare students for the next grade level.

The principal maintains an accountability sheet that tracks student progress so teachers and curriculum facilitators can work together to adjust teaching practice to address specific gaps at the individual student or curriculum level (e.g., measurement in math).

(Continued)

(Continued)

The school has also contracted with a curriculum management system that tracks individual student progress across grade levels. Despite high poverty, limited English proficiency, and high mobility, LCE students are considered among the best students in the district when they move on to the middle school level.

Lackland's success in advancing equity and excellence in student learning has occurred through the establishment of a shared vision, data-driven problem setting, the development and implementation of evidence-based plans, assessment of results, and reflection on how to refine their strategies to continue to move forward.

SOURCE: Lackland City Elementary School. From Allen, J., Meza, M. E., Billnitzer, K. (2008). "Developing Attitudes for Success." Presentation to the UW-Madison Wisconsin Idea Leadership Academy Conference, July 7–10.

Developing Teacher Capacity

The first process dimension of leadership for learning is developing teacher capacity, a core strategy for improving student learning. Ironically, despite the fact that the quality of teaching is the primary factor that determines student success in learning, many schools focus insufficient attention on the development of teachers and teaching practice. This chapter examines the ways in which socio-cognitive leadership can advance teacher capacity of the school and thereby advance learning for all students.

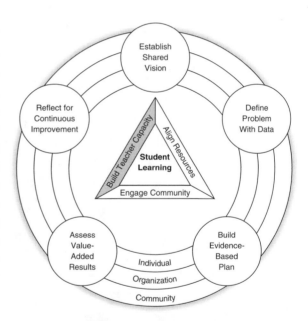

Guiding Questions

- How have you worked to build teacher capacity to meet student needs and raise student achievement?
- How have you worked to build a professional learning community with high expectations and accountability for the improvement of teaching and learning?
- How have you worked to support *all* teachers, including teachers who struggle, to grow professionally and engage in reflective practice?

The impact of teacher quality on student learning cannot be overstated. William Sanders and his colleagues (Sanders & Rivers, 1996) developed a statistical procedure to estimate the effects of having a strong teacher—one whose students make large learning gains during the school year—compared to the effects of having a weak teacher—one whose students make small learning gains. Students in strong teachers' classrooms make significantly higher gains in learning, and these effects are cumulative. In other words, if students are lucky enough to be assigned to a good teacher three years in a row, they build a huge learning advantage over their peers who started with similar achievement levels but were assigned to lower quality teachers. The size of the effect is staggering. After three years of effective math instruction, fifth-grade students scored at the 83rd percentile, while children *with the same initial test scores* assigned to three ineffective teachers in a row scored at the 29th percentile.

Another study by Jordan, Mendro, and Weerasinghe (1997) found similar results. The average reading scores of Dallas fourth graders assigned to three effective teachers in a row rose from the 59th percentile in fourth grade to the 76th percentile by the conclusion of sixth grade. Students assigned to ineffective teachers during the same time period saw declines from the 60th percentile in fourth grade to the 42nd percentile in sixth grade. These studies provide tangible proof of what we all know: Teaching has a *huge* effect on student learning and can determine whether students succeed or fail in school.

So, we know that teacher effectiveness matters. But how do we measure and advance teacher capacity? It turns out to be somewhat difficult to explain teacher effectiveness through common measures of teacher preparation and experience. In a review of the research literature, Jennifer King Rice (2003) found that teacher experience, completing a teacher preparation program and degree, teacher certification in the subject, teacher coursework, and test scores are all related to teacher effectiveness, but not surprisingly, a large proportion of the variance in teacher effectiveness remains unexplained by these variables.

The best way to measure teaching effectiveness is to examine teaching itself. In the remainder of the chapter, we consider how schools that close achievement gaps and improve learning for all students use socio-cognitive leadership to advance teaching and learning by focusing on defining, measuring, and developing strong teaching practice. Figure 6.1 provides an overview of the process of advancing teacher capacity through socio-cognitive leadership.

Figure 6.1 Advancing Teacher Capacity Through Socio-Cognitive Leadership

1. Begin with a clear, shared vision of the preferred state: What will good teaching look like in the curricular and social context of this school?

2. Collaboratively examine data on teaching practice and student learning to assess teacher capacity: What do teachers currently know and do?

3. Develop evidence-based plans to advance teacher capacity and embed problem-solving and teacher development in the work of teachers: How can we strengthen teaching practices that best support student learning?

4. Examine teaching practice and student outcomes to assess growth in teacher capacity: How have teaching and learning improved as a result of the plan?

5. Consider areas for further improvement, and build on successful strategies to continue to strengthen teaching and learning in the school: How can we refine our strategy to continue to improve teacher effectiveness?

ESTABLISH THE SHARED VISION OR PREFERRED STATE

The first stage in advancing teacher capacity is to work together as a school community to develop a clear vision of the preferred state. In other words, what does good teaching practice look like? In order for teachers and others to work toward continually strengthening and advancing teaching practice, there needs to be a clear, shared understanding of what that preferred state would look like. When teachers close their eyes and imagine an ideal classroom or an ideal teaching situation, they should have a shared understanding of what that would look like. More specifically, those who teach in the same subject should share an understanding of effective content-based pedagogy: Math teachers should share an understanding of what an effective algebra lesson might look like. And yet, in most schools, there is no shared understanding and very limited communication among teachers and staff about what exceptional teaching practice really is.

To establish that shared vision, school leaders need to have a clear picture of excellent teaching practice, and the leadership team needs to develop regular opportunities for conversations among teachers about what that practice looks like. The successful schools we have observed often foster these conversations through the reallocation of resources to hire instructional coaches. The coaches carry a consistent vision of excellent teaching practice to each classroom and facilitate conversations among staff to clarify and embed the vision across teaching staff.

Two books that capture the vision of teaching excellence present in *Learning First* schools are *How People Learn: Brain, Mind, Experience, and School,* by Bransford, Brown, and Cocking (1999), and *Preparing Teachers for a Changing World: What Teachers Should Learn and Be Able to Do,* by Darling-Hammond and Bransford (2005).

Both books build on research concerning learning and cognition that recognizes that all learning is social, and learning is based on experience. Effective learning environments exist within a community context, and they are learner centered, knowledge centered, and assessment centered. These elements lead to the importance of teacher knowledge to establish the key elements of an effective learning environment:

- student centered,
- knowledge centered,
- assessment centered, and
- community centered.

How People Learn (1999) and *Preparing Teachers for a Changing World* (2005) are philosophically consistent with the work of the National Board for Professional Teaching Standards and Danielson's *Enhancing Professional Practice: A Framework for Teaching* (2007), a teacher evaluation framework developed to provide formative feedback to teachers to enhance and extend teaching practice. In our experience, schools that support teachers in pursuing National Board Certification and districts adopting the Danielson *Framework* also create opportunities for conversation, clarification, and the development of shared understanding about what it means to be a good teacher.

Districts can also play an important role in developing a clear definition of good teaching. The Kennewick School District in Kennewick, Washington, has developed clear, shared understanding of what the district defines as effective teaching. This vision of effective teaching—shown in Figure 6.2—was developed by teachers and is shared and reinforced through district walk-throughs of schools. The district office established a goal that central office employees are expected to be in the schools at least 10 hours a week to provide a presence and to reinforce a shared vision of effective teaching.

Another approach to establishing a vision of good teaching is one taken by the Madison Metropolitan School District in Madison, Wisconsin. The district has developed a set of research-based instructional tools around the teaching of literacy and mathematics that provide clear direction around teaching and learning in specific content areas. These materials are discussed more fully in Chapter 10.

Figure 6.2   Kennewick School District Vision of Effective Teaching

The Kennewick School District holds as its highest priority supporting the professional growth of its staff so that every classroom provides the maximum learning experience for each student. We also believe that clarity and focus provide a strong foundation for growth. To that end, a task force of teachers and administrators was formed to define and describe the essential core of what effective teaching and learning is in our district. While this document does not attempt to include every element and dynamic of teaching and learning, it does intend to clarify four critical components:

PURPOSE   **ENGAGEMENT**   **RIGOR**   **RESULTS**

It is important that the document is seen in support of *growth* of *all* teachers and *all* instructional leaders. It is not intended as a tool for judgment or evaluation.

It is the hope of the task force that this document will provide *talking points*, which will support a wide variety of professional development activities, including the following:

- Learning walks
- Self-reflection
- Video labs of classroom interactions
- Focus for staff meeting dialogues
- Tool for peer coaching and peer mentoring
- Teacher-to-teacher collaboration

PURPOSE: Teacher intentionally plans and instructs for student achievement of essential learnings.

Teacher Indicators	Guiding Questions	Student Indicators
Clearly sets and reinforces outcome throughout the lesson; links activities to the outcome.	How does the identified outcome guide the learning?	Can explain what they are learning and why.
Supports students in making connections to prior learning and life situations.	How is the learning made relevant to students?	Applies learning in different settings and situations.
Prioritizes instructional strategies according to student needs.	How are learning activities appropriately matched to student needs?	Demonstrates understanding of concepts and mastery of skills.
Has and communicates a clear plan for assessing student work.	How does assessment help frame the learning?	Understands how his or her work will be assessed.

(Continued)

(Continued)

ENGAGEMENT: Teacher and students actively participate in the learning and are focused on the lesson.

Teacher Indicators	Guiding Questions	Student Indicators
Facilitates discussion, monitors learning activities, and stimulates interest in learning.	How is participation demonstrated?	Asks and responds to questions, completes assignments, contributes to discussions.
Shows joy and passion for learning.	What is the evidence of motivation?	Shows persistence and enthusiasm for learning.
Seeks feedback, analyzes his or her work, and uses reflection to inform next steps of learning.	In what ways is reflection part of the classroom routine?	Seeks feedback, evaluates his or her work; uses reflection to deepen understanding.
Tries new instructional strategies, demonstrates being a learner.	How is risk-taking modeled?	Shares his or her thinking and work, participates in new learning experiences.

RIGOR: Each learner develops higher levels of thinking through content that is complex, ambiguous, provocative, and personally challenging.

Teacher Indicators	Guiding Questions	Student Indicators
Varies question type, uses wait time, and asks higher level questions.	How do questions support student learning?	Gives thoughtful responses, asks meaningful questions.
Builds to more complex concepts, anticipates likely confusions, reteaches and provides enrichment as appropriate.	How does the content of the lesson provide the correct level of difficulty?	Challenged by new concepts, builds on prior learning, and learns from mistakes.
Intentionally builds conceptual knowledge, chooses to cover less breadth for more depth.	What is the evidence of deeper understanding?	Synthesizes, analyzes, generalizes thinking.
Stresses student responsibility and accountability, accepts only quality work, consistently encourages all students.	How are high expectations an influence on learning?	Produces quality work, demonstrates willingness to *rewrite* and/or *redo*.

RESULTS: The intended learning is achieved.

Teacher Indicators	Guiding Questions	Student Indicators
Creates opportunities for students to demonstrate learning, gives timely feedback.	How is student understanding monitored?	Completes learning tasks, uses vocabulary, and demonstrates mastery of skills.
Uses multiple measures over time to gather data.	How are assessments used to evaluate learning?	Completes a variety of assessments.
Evaluates results and adjusts instruction both for groups and individual students.	How is data used to improve performance?	Sets personal learning goals.

SOURCE: Kennewick School District. From Lindbloom, M., Fancher, G., Rosier, P. (2007). "Quality Instruction Isn't Everything, It's the Only Thing," Presentation to the UW-Madison Wisconsin Idea Leadership Academy Conference, July 8–12. Used with permission.

Each of these approaches defines effective teaching to be consistent with research on learning and cognition, emphasizing teaching that has the following characteristics:

- Learner centered: Constructivist, differentiates instruction, engages students, builds on student understanding and experience; focuses on addressing student needs, scaffolds advanced learning, fosters mastery learning
- Knowledge centered: Builds disciplinary language and understanding using higher-level teaching
- Assessment centered: Assesses for common errors or misperceptions, provides focused formative feedback to pinpoint learning and learning needs, holds teachers accountable through summative assessments
- Community centered: Builds supportive and respectful relationships to improve student learning both inside and outside the classroom

DEFINE THE PROBLEM WITH DATA

With the preferred state defined and the vision of effective teaching shared among teachers, the socio-cognitive leadership framework moves next to developing a data profile of existing teacher capacity and a strength assessment of the existing teaching force, including the identification of strong instructional leaders who can help to move the school toward its vision of teaching excellence.

Figure 6.3 is a teacher capacity audit that shows the types of data that should be considered in identifying current strengths in teaching and vision gaps.

Figure 6.3   Audit Guide: Developing Teacher Capacity

Step 1: Understand the Baseline

What is the distribution of teachers, recent historical trends, and expected future trends concerning the following?

- Teacher demographics (career stage, race, gender)
- Teacher turnover
- Staff assignments
- Education level and focus; certifications/licensure areas
- Teacher knowledge, expertise, and key contributions
- Perceived teaching strengths and areas in need of further development
- Staff leadership experience and capabilities
- Training and recognition/National Board Certifications

Step 2: Examine Disaggregated Outcomes

What are the patterns in student learning organized by student access to quality teaching? Continue this analysis until you have a clear understanding of the gaps between the vision of access to high quality teaching/challenging curriculum for all students and the current reality (the vision gap). Disaggregate by pedagogy, curriculum units/content, courses, departments, grade levels, programs, teacher or leadership teams.

- What settings produce the highest levels of *student learning and engagement*? For students who succeed at high levels, what are the course-taking or programming patterns? What curriculum are these students exposed to?
- What settings produce the highest levels of *teacher success* in terms of value-added student learning, teacher retention, and continuous improvement in teaching practice?
- What settings produce the lowest levels of student learning? For students who perform at the lowest levels, what are the course-taking or programming patterns? What curriculum are these students exposed to?
- What are the patterns of behavioral disruptions, discipline, and referrals? (Who is referred, in what context, by whom, for what reason?)

Step 3: Analyze Current Practices

Examine current practices that support teacher growth and effectiveness.

Teaching Practice

- What current instructional practices are particularly effective?
- What are staff practices in relation to inclusion, differentiated instruction, flexible grouping, and student engagement?

- How does the staff work to address individual student learning needs for disengaged students, engaged students, and advanced students?
- What is the quality and availability of curricular materials? What curricular materials produce highest levels of student learning, and what materials do teachers routinely struggle with, sidestep, or adapt?
- How does staff use available books, libraries, and technologies?

Capacity Building

- What types of feedback, both formal and informal, serve as a catalyst for improved practice, for novice through expert teachers, and what sources have limited utility in advancing teacher capacity?
- How are professional development and other resources deployed to ensure a focus on the most critical areas for improving teaching and learning?
- Are current staff development opportunities job embedded, long term, and content focused with opportunities for active learning and guided practice?
- What leadership opportunities and organizational structures exist to support instructional leadership by teachers as leaders, mentors, coaches, team members, and department chairs?

Step 4: Consider Common Problems in Advancing Teacher Capacity That May Need to Be Addressed

- Does the staff share a common vision of what an effective classroom looks like? Is there an explicit model of good teaching?
- What are the sources of regular teacher feedback that are effective in improving instructional practice (e.g., walk-throughs, instructional coaching, collaborative problem solving with other teachers, team teaching, evaluation, supervision, formative assessment)?
- Are professional development resources targeted to evidence-based practice that addresses the vision gap?
- How are student and class assignments made? Is attention paid to ensuring balanced student assignment practices that support teacher growth and student learning?
- What incentives are in place to encourage professional growth (compensation, recognition, support for conferences, school visits, and classroom observations)?

Step 5: Answer Summary Questions

- How have you worked to build teacher capacity to meet student needs and raise student achievement?
- How have you worked to build a professional learning community with high expectations and accountability for the improvement of teaching and learning?
- How have you worked to support *all* teachers, including teachers who struggle, to grow professionally and engage in reflective practice?

The audit begins with baseline data analysis of the teaching force. The purpose is to understand the current capacity of teachers, including strengths as well as challenges, the experience levels, and likely ongoing stability of the teaching force. Some aspects of understanding the baseline and examining student outcomes may be perceived to be evaluative, so school leaders need to consider this in deciding who should be involved in conducting the audit and how much of the data will be shared. Regardless, an honest evaluation of teacher capacity is needed to consider how teachers are currently being supported, what kinds of professional support and accountability measures may be needed to strengthen teaching practices, and what vision gaps exist between current teaching practice and the preferred state.

The second step in the process is to disaggregate teacher data by student outcomes. Again, these data may present political challenges, as school cultures are not always conducive to disaggregating data about student learning by teacher or classroom. In some cases, the principal may need to conduct this analysis independently or with a small, trusted leadership team and gradually move to build a shared understanding of the teacher capacity vision gap. To move this process forward, principals often work individually with teachers or in small groups, such as grade-level teams, to get teachers accustomed to seeing student achievement feedback structured by classroom before these data are more widely shared. In the interim, data can be disaggregated by subject, grade level, or student demographics to inform shared problems in teacher capacity across the school. Ultimately, the goal is to be more transparent about teacher strengths and learning needs, so that teachers can work together to address challenging problems of practice.

A critical element of advancing teacher capacity is the development of professional learning communities or communities of practice among teachers that work together to develop, implement, and refine effective teaching practice. Communities of practice form when there is a clear, shared vision of a desired state; there is a clear understanding of gaps in achieving that state; and there is a shared belief that by working together, we can move forward toward that preferred state more effectively than if we worked alone. A more complete discussion of communities of practice occurs in Chapter 8, but it is important here to note that communities of practice support teacher learning and motivate teachers to work together to address problems of practice.

Sherman Middle School in Madison, Wisconsin, is a diverse urban school that has closed the achievement gap between its large Hispanic English as a Second Language population and white students in the district. It is also an example of a school that has invested in a focused effort at building teacher capacity. The school has succeeded by establishing clear goals and hiring and building a teaching force that is committed to social justice and the education of all of its students. Figure 6.4 is adapted from an instrument developed by Sherman Middle School to advance

Figure 6.4   Looking at Teacher Work

This protocol asks you to reflect on your use of various activities and methods that are associated with high quality learning and relationships. It is assumed that individuals and teams follow normal modes of instruction, such as whole-group instruction; the items in the protocol focus on extending curriculum and teaching beyond standard methods.

The process involves two steps. First, complete the chart individually. Then the team or group should complete it while discussing the individual responses. At the end of the session each team will be asked to put their forms in an envelope and mark it in some way only they could identify. These can be held for revisiting at a later date.

Please use the following keys for completing the chart.

Scale for "How Often"	Key for "Who Does"	Key for "Intentionality"
5—Daily 4—Weekly 3—Once per Month 2—Once per Quarter 1—Not at All	I—One teacher does this, but not the whole team together I/T—One teacher plans this for the whole team to use T—The whole team plans and implements this	U (Unintentional)—This was done through serendipitous or accidental use (e.g., "Well, that activity sort of involved some student voice or subject integration."). P (Planned)—This was done intentionally and explicitly after planning by the team.

Looking at Teacher Work

Activities and Methods	How Often Is This Done?	Who Does This?	Is It Intentional?	Notes
Specific work on building relationships and community within a group or team				
Flexible grouping for differentiation				
Structured opportunities for students to work in teams with other students				
Problem solving to address a specific student's learning needs				
Alternative assessments and projects for differentiation				

(Continued)

(Continued)

Activities and Methods	How Often Is This Done?	Who Does This?	Is It Intentional?	Notes
Identification and support for students who need more time and support to succeed				
Intentional use of integrative themes or projects				
Classroom writing assignments with Six Traits instruction				
Teacher-led discussions on current events or content-related topics including Socratic discussions				
Assessment of student work to inform instruction/lesson development				
Teacher-student collaborative planning of curriculum or activities				
Journal writing for self-reflection and assessment				
Interviews of individual students by teachers				
Identification of curricular scope and sequence				
Clearly defined outcome expectations for students for the unit or course				
Use of library media center for guided research on projects				
Use of technology/ computer lab				

SOURCE: Sherman Elementary School. From Yehle, Anne et al., "The Sherman Way: Advancing Learning for Our Students, Staff and Families." Presentation at the UW-Madison Wisconsin Idea Leadership Academy Conference, July 8–12. Used with permission.

teaching practice by focusing on the current context for teaching in the school and to engage teacher teams in reflection about the degree to which they used *high value* curriculum and teaching practice.

Leaders of schools that continuously improve and address the needs of all learners focus much of their leadership effort on ensuring that the school is a learning organization, and that a primary area of learning and advancement is the quality of teaching that occurs in the school. These effective leaders continuously strive to grow their human resources through careful hiring, advocating for district resources to support needed staffing, reallocating resources to provide coaching and other professional development opportunities, and providing continuous, informal feedback to teachers to put them in a mindset to want to continuously work to hone their teaching skills.

Specifically, three primary areas of focus advance teacher capacity: *advancing pedagogical knowledge* and use of teaching strategies to meet individual student needs and raise achievement levels; *building communities of practice* among teachers to support collaborative problem solving, professional growth, and teacher development; and *working to ensure that all teachers are supported* to grow professionally and engage in reflective practice, including but not limited to the teachers who struggle the most in their teaching practice.

BUILD AN EVIDENCE-BASED PLAN

Once the school has collected and examined data to understand the strengths and gaps in teacher capacity, teachers may begin to work together to identify evidence-based strategies that address vision gaps. Figure 6.5 provides examples of teacher-development strategies used by schools that have succeeded in closing achievement gaps and advancing learning for all students.

Socio-Cognitive Leadership

Schools that put learning first use the socio-cognitive leadership process to establish a clear vision of excellence in teaching that drives teacher recruitment, development, and accountability. Many of the schools we worked with operated in large, urban school districts, which had strong union rules about teacher transfer. In these districts, some principals felt constrained by contractual rules to accept teacher transfers even if the teacher did not share the school's vision. But in the schools that put learning first, principals understood how to translate the vision into a set of clear and high expectations for teachers in the interview

Figure 6.5   Common Evidence-Based Interventions to Build Teacher Capacity

Socio-Cognitive Leadership

- Shared vision of effective teaching drives recruitment, development, and accountability of teachers
- Teacher capacity audit; collaborative data analysis and planning
- Research-based or evidence-based plans
- Value-added assessment of results
- Reflection and a commitment to continuous improvement

Building Communities of Practice

- Common planning time and common assessments
- Leader and peer walk-throughs

Supporting All Teachers to Grow Professionally

- Professional development
- Behavior management system and tools
- Instructional coaches
- Shared videos and analysis of instruction
- Formative assessment of student learning
- Evaluation, mentoring, and support
- Team teaching
- Team training for professional development
- National Board Certification

Accountability and Feedback

- Framework for teacher evaluation system
  - Goal setting
  - 360 degree evaluation
- Incentives and compensation
- Recognition and support for risk-taking
- Hiring and selection practices

process. In effect, teachers self-selected into or out of the school depending on their commitment to the vision of the school and their willingness to work to achieve it.

In one case after an interview, the principal called a teacher who was about to use her seniority rights to transfer into the school and said, "By contract, you have every right to come here, but this is what we expect, and frankly, I don't think you are committed to working as hard as we work here in a collaborative team. I don't think you can do it." The principal told us that the teacher didn't back down. She said that she was committed to working collaboratively to achieve the vision. In the end, she came to the school and worked hard to live up to the high standards set for her. In other cases, the principal told us that after an interview, many teachers eligible for transfer would decide that they weren't committed enough to the vision to work that hard, and they chose not to transfer to the school.

Building Communities of Practice

The *Learning First* schools also support the development of strong communities of practice among teachers. The teachers share an understanding of the vision gap and a commitment to implementing the evidence-based plan by working together to achieve the vision. Structural supports, such as common planning time, provide opportunities for teachers to work together to solve critical problems of practice. In addition, in many *Learning First* schools, leaders support and model problem solving with teachers using feedback from common assessments and leader or teacher walk-throughs.

Supporting All Teachers to Grow Professionally

The strength of the teaching force in *Learning First* schools is no accident. These schools provide structural supports to strengthen teaching practice, including long-term, job-embedded professional development such as through the use of instructional coaches who are permanent, full-time members of the school staff; analysis of teaching videos; formative assessments; and team-teaching opportunities.

Accountability and Feedback

Learning First schools hold teachers, teacher mentors, and the administrative team accountable for teacher induction and support of high quality teaching practice. Accountability can be formal or informal, but teachers know what is expected of them, and they are held accountable for continuously working to strengthen teaching and learning.

Figure 6.6 provides an example of a tool that could be used to assess and provide feedback on teacher-classroom practice as part of a walk-through strategy. In walk-throughs, administrators or teachers visit classrooms on a routine basis, spending a short period of time (three to five minutes) in the classroom, making notes about the lesson and providing some quick feedback to teachers about their work. Walk-throughs provide an example of a common tool that is used to build community (as walk-throughs generate opportunities for conversations about teaching practice), provide feedback, and hold teachers accountable.

Many schools and districts have developed walk-through documents to guide these brief observations and reflections. Ideally, the walk-through document reflects the shared vision of teaching practice and addresses areas identified as goals for advancing teaching practice in the school. Walk-through protocols are usually used by school administrators, but the schools and districts we have worked with have also used them for central office administrator walk-throughs (Kennewick, Washington), and teacher walk-throughs (Dayton's Bluff Elementary School in St. Paul, Minnesota). Walk-through *look-fors* may thus be developed collaboratively by teachers at the school level or by district-level administrators trying to foster a common shared understanding of effective teaching practice across the district. Figure 6.6 provides an example of a walk-through document developed by the teachers and the principal at West Ridge Elementary School to guide feedback about teaching practice from administrator and teacher walk-throughs.

ASSESS VALUE-ADDED RESULTS AND REFLECT FOR CONTINUOUS IMPROVEMENT

Teacher capacity, like student learning, is an area for ongoing focus and continuous improvement. Periodic assessment of teacher learning provides guidance for refining, refocusing, and renewing capacity-building efforts. Teacher learning can be assessed by examining teaching practice such as through the use of walk-throughs and feedback from formal teacher evaluation. Instructional coaches can also provide an important source of information about areas of successful implementation and areas needing further professional development, opportunities for collaboration, and planning and implementation. A second mechanism for assessing teacher learning is to examine *student* learning—student test score data and outcomes, particularly assessed through value-added measures. These sources of data can be compared with existing strategies for improvement, and leaders can refine approaches to continually advance teacher learning.

In the next section, we describe the case of Schenk Elementary School, which provides an example of a school that used a strong shared vision and a focus on teacher and student learning to advance professional learning communities and teacher capacity using the socio-cognitive leadership lens.

Figure 6.6   Walk-Through Worksheet

Guiding Questions	Reflection
Student Achievement • Is flexible grouping evident? • How is the purpose of the lesson clearly stated? • How does assessment frame the lesson and flexible grouping? Other Comments:	
Student Engagement • How does the teacher engage the students? • Why are the children motivated? • Is student reflection part of the routine? • How are all students encouraged to engage? Other Comments:	
Rigor • How do questions support student learning? • What is evidence of deeper understanding? • How are high expectations an influence on learning? Other Comments:	
Operational Efficiency • How is the classroom organized efficiently for instruction? • How is the classroom organized efficiently for operational management? Other Comments:	

SOURCE: Used with permission of Matt Geiger.

Example: Schenk Elementary School

Sheila Briggs was principal of Schenk Elementary, a diverse urban neighborhood school in the Midwest. When she arrived at Schenk, she found a school with strong community support but teachers with low morale and weak academic expectations. The school had achieved a reputation in the district as a nice place to work, and some teachers transferred to the school expecting a less demanding work environment. Principal Briggs oversaw a major turnaround in the school, bringing the school from low levels of proficient performance in third-grade reading to 100% proficiency in a five-year period. Her strategy was to establish a strong professional learning community driven by a shared vision of student learning, drawing from DuFour's (1998, 2006, 2008) work on professional community. Briggs energized the community by getting them to envision a different future for Schenk and by creating clear expectations that teachers would participate in an active learning community focused on improving learning for all students.

Teachers who shared the vision for a strong community of teachers pursuing high levels of student learning were active in the school. Principal Briggs set clear expectations in the hiring process for participation in professional development and the emerging professional community. She used the baseline data analysis to provide data to support a grant application, which enabled her to hire an instructional coach in reading and to provide additional professional development for teachers. The school moved quickly to having a reputation as a school on the move, and energetic and committed teachers requested transfers to the school to become a part of the thriving professional community. Some teachers who were not prepared for the change in culture opted to leave for *easier* schools.

Teachers, parents, and other stakeholders came together to develop a new vision for the school. They started by responding to the prompt, "It is the year 2008. Schenk just won an award for the best school in the country. What made it that way?" After lots of brainstorming and narrowing down and combining, the group developed a vision that detailed teacher, student, parent, and community commitment to moving the school forward.

Principal Briggs used the district's balanced literacy framework—described in Chapter 10—to support the development of a strong, shared vision of effective literacy instruction. Teachers in the school took ownership of the framework and used it daily in literacy instruction.

SOURCE: UW Madison Master Administrator Capstone Certificate Portfolio Document. Used with permission of Lisa Kvistad.

Managing and Aligning Resources

Chapters 5 and 6 have described how leaders advance *student learning* and *teacher learning* through socio-cognitive leadership. Specifically, socio-cognitive leaders build communities of practice that advance student and teacher learning by establishing a commitment to a shared vision of the preferred state, by using data to understand and set the problem, by developing and implementing an evidence-based plan, by using data to assess the results, and by reflecting on these results to retool the vision and the

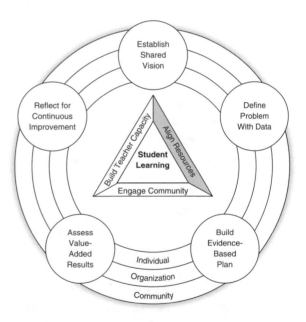

Guiding Questions

- How have you aligned all resources (financial, human, and physical resources) to advance the vision of equity and excellence in the school or district?
- How have you acquired and managed resources to address learning inequities in your school or district?
- How have you worked to ensure a safe and secure learning environment for students and staff?

plan in order to move the organization forward. This chapter focuses on a third dimension of leadership—*managing and aligning resources* to advance equity and excellence in student learning.

Resources provide an interesting challenge for putting learning first because often, educators view the existing resource mix—including financial, human, and physical resources—as inadequate and fixed. There is never enough, and what is there is already allocated in ways that are historically or externally determined and inflexible. Educational leaders that advance equity and excellence in student learning do not assume that the existing resource mix is fixed, but instead they put student learning at the center and consider what resources they can add to the mix and what resources can be used more wisely to advance student learning goals.

Figure 7.1 provides an overview of socio-cognitive leadership as applied to managing resources to put learning first.

Figure 7.1   Managing Resources Through Socio-Cognitive Leadership

1. Begin with a clear, shared vision of the preferred state: What will effective management of financial, human, and physical capital look like given the goals for improving teaching and learning in this school?

2. Collaboratively examine resource data to understand the impact of current allocation of resources on teaching practice and student learning: How are resources currently distributed, and what are the consequences for advancing equity and excellence in student learning?

3. Develop evidence-based plans to acquire, manage, and reallocate resources to address vision gaps: How can resources be better used to support the school's learning goals?

4. Examine changes in student learning outcomes as a result of the reallocation of resources: How have teaching and learning improved as a result of the plan?

5. Consider areas for further improvement and build on successful strategies to continue to target resource use in the school: How can we refine our strategy to continue to improve school effectiveness?

In order to advance a vision for a preferred state in resource management, we consider Maslow's Hierarchy of Needs. Maslow (1943) identifies foundational needs that must be addressed in order to realize higher order needs and achieve self-actualization. In our vision, schools that put learning first ensure that foundational needs are met in order to advance student and teacher learning needs. In doing so, they ensure that basic needs (physiological and safety) and social needs (love, belonging, and esteem) are met so that the school can address and meet learning needs (self-actualization). Because the learning environment is most effective when all three levels of needs—basic, social, and learning needs—are adequately addressed, the vision for managing and aligning resources is to acquire, allocate, and reallocate resources to ensure a solid foundation for learning to occur. Therefore, the basic-social-learning needs typology provides a foundation and focus for vision setting, data analysis, planning, assessing, and reflecting on the management and alignment of school resources.

Schools that put learning first have effective processes in place for acquiring, allocating, and aligning three types of resources:

- Financial resources
- Human resources
- Physical resources

The next sections provide information and tools on how to assess the current allocation of resources and strategies for more effective resource management. In doing so, we use the socio-cognitive framework to advance resource management.

FINANCIAL RESOURCES

Research suggests that resource allocation in schools can be designed to support effective strategies to enable all students to learn to high levels. By identifying effective strategies and interventions that support student learning, resource allocation can be connected to the broader vision of advancing learning for all students.

Establishing the Shared Vision or Preferred State

In *Learning First* schools, resource limitations do not impede progress. In addition to fund-raising acumen, the creativity and skill that effective resource managers display also includes understanding creative ways to use financial resources more effectively to grease the skids—to motivate, reward, compensate, and finance evidence-based plans to acquire, allocate, and align resources in ways that enable the school to achieve its collective vision.

Thus, the vision for the management and alignment of financial resources is to obtain adequate resources to fund evidence-based intervention strategies to achieve the vision of equity and excellence in student learning.

Define the Problem With Data

Figure 7.2 provides guiding questions and areas for focus in data collection and analysis as it relates to financial resources. The audit guide begins by putting the resource base in context: How do school-level resources compare to state averages or comparable schools? This comparative analysis provides the school leader with information regarding resource adequacy that can provide an important perspective about the need to strongly advocate for additional resources to address deficits. Alternatively, the comparative analysis may show that the school has adequate resources, and the problem of financial management should focus more heavily on resource reallocation rather than resource acquisition.

Figure 7.2   Audit Guide: Managing and Aligning Financial Resources

Step 1: Understand the Baseline

What is the current distribution of school financial resources?

- What financial resources are available to your school compared to state averages or comparable schools?
- Considering all of the financial resources available for your school, what resources are discretionary, what do you have influence over, and what do you have no control over?
- How are you currently spending your discretionary resources?
- What financial resources are available that are not reflected in the school budget? Consider grant opportunities, business sponsorships, parent and community organizations, and students.

Step 2: Examine Disaggregated Outcomes

What is the relationship between the allocation of resources and teaching and learning outcomes? Continue this analysis until you have a clear understanding of the gaps between the vision for resources targeted to student learning needs and the current reality (the vision gap).

- What groups of students are achieving, and what groups are failing?
- What financial resources are allocated to achieving students? What resources are allocated to failing students? (Consider class sizes, allocation of experienced or effective teachers, academic enrichment programming, etc.)
- What remedial, behavioral, engagement, relationship building, language acquisition, and emotional support services are associated with improved student outcomes?

For middle and high schools,

- What groups of students are engaged and what groups are not engaged?
- What financial resources are allocated to engaged students? What resources are allocated to students who are not engaged?

Step 3: Analyze Current Practices

Examine the current management and allocation of resources to promote growth in student learning.

- How are financial resources (class size, instructional time, extended time, curricular resources, and technology) used to improve student achievement and engagement?
- Is there a process in place to expand and extend the current financial resources to promote growth in student learning?

Step 4: Consider Common Problems in Allocating Resources That May Need to Be Addressed

- Does the vision for equity and excellence in student learning drive the use of financial resources in the school?
- Are decisions about the allocation of resources based on maintaining job security and the status quo in order to minimize inconvenience to teachers?
- Is a regular process in place to assess the value added from resource investments?
- Is there a process in place to abandon past practices that do not target critical need areas and redirect resources to advance equity and excellence in student learning?
- Is there a process in place to identify and expose resource gaps and advocate for resources to address those gaps?

Step 5: Answer Summary Questions

- How have you aligned financial resources to advance the vision of equity and excellence in the school or district?
- How have you acquired and managed resources to address learning inequities in your school or district?
- How have worked to ensure a safe and secure learning environment for students and staff?

The audit focuses on all resources to provide a holistic picture of the budget. Often, school leaders consider only discretionary resources, but in the schools we worked with, we found that principals that put learning first often leveraged political capital for additional district resources. In addition, these master principals knew how and where to tap the community for needed funds to provide student incentive prizes or obtain sponsorship for a new initiative. They were rarely held back by resource constraints and found creative ways to obtain additional resources to advance student learning. Furthermore, these principals turned down resources that would require them to invest in activities that distracted from the shared vision.

Next, the financial resource audit focuses on current resource allocations as investments and examines student outcomes that result from these investments. What programs provide significant learning gains for students? What activities provide limited support for student learning?

Can resources be better spent to advance student engagement and learning? What is the vision gap?

Build an Evidence-Based Plan

The collaborative analysis of resources provides a clear understanding of the current resource mix and the sources and uses of existing funds. The next step in the process is to determine an evidence-based plan and identify areas of the budget that might need reallocation or additional resources that should be sought to extend the resource base. The specific uses of funds will be determined by the vision gap identified in the learning funnel analysis (see Chapter 3) given the specific problems that have been identified as critical areas of focus to ensure adequately and effectively managed resources to advance student learning.

While the specific strategies to be undertaken need to be determined through collaborative analysis of local data, research provides some general guidance for funding strategies that support evidence-based plans to advance student learning. Building on the research on effective strategies to advance student learning, Figure 7.3 provides examples of evidence-based

Figure 7.3   Common Evidence-Based Interventions for Managing and Aligning Financial Resources

---

Socio-Cognitive Leadership

- Shared vision of high-level learning for all students
- Resource audit
- Evidence-based plan for instructional materials and methods
- Value-added assessment of results
- Reflection and a commitment to continuous improvement

Reallocate Human and Financial Resources

- Investment in professional development
- Subject-area instructional coaches
- Time during the school day for collaborative work
- Classroom and school visits to observe best practices
- Reduced elementary class sizes

Extra Time for Learning

- Tutoring
- Extended day
- Summer school
- Formative student assessments

Acquiring Additional Resources

- Grant funds
- Foundation support
- Business partnerships
- Private donors

interventions for managing and aligning financial resources with a vision of advancing equity and excellence in student learning. Some of the examples derive from research on resource allocation and reallocation by Odden and Archibald (2008) and Miles and Frank (2007). These authors argue that by studying the budget allocation decisions of schools that have successfully doubled performance, one can identify resource use patterns (including support for teacher professional development) that support learning environments that provide opportunities for all students to learn to high levels.

There is a growing evidence base regarding effective allocation of resources to promote student achievement. Some of these include smaller class sizes for students in the early elementary grades and subject-area instructional coaches, who provide a regular presence in the school providing ideas, suggestions, and modeling effective teaching practices. Another important use of resources is buying time for teachers to work together to align curriculum, develop common assessments, problem solve, share information about student learning needs, and to obtain training or learn about new approaches through classroom observations of other teachers or site visits to other schools.

Buying time for students is also an important investment. Students who are unable to master the material in the allotted time need extra time to enable them to master challenging content. In *Learning First* schools, financial resources are allocated to the purchase of learning time for students—additional support before, after, and during school; on Saturdays; and in the summer.

Resources can also buy information. Many schools are beginning to invest in formative assessments that provide immediate, clear feedback on student progress. The information from these formative assessments provides feedback to teachers about student progress in real time so they can adjust learning strategies and reteach as necessary to ensure that all students are able to master critical content.

Assess Value-Added Results and Reflect for Continuous Improvement

Leaders that put learning first view financial resources as an asset and not a constraint to advance student learning. Virtually all of the *Learning First* schools we have studied and worked with have applied discretionary resources to advance student learning. They are successful grant writers and fund raisers, and they network with district-level personnel to become aware of and to acquire discretionary resources available at the district level.

School leaders who reallocate resources should determine in advance what the expected impact of shifts in resources will be in order to be able to assess the effectiveness of new resource distributions. Thus, the development of a plan for resource management and alignment should be accompanied by a clear understanding of baseline data and expected outcomes so that the allocation of resources can be assessed using clear benchmarked expectations of the results. These assessment data should be revisited periodically and reflected upon to assess needs and to guide future efforts at resource acquisition, allocation, and alignment of financial resources.

HUMAN RESOURCES

A second category of resources that is skillfully managed by leaders in schools that close achievement gaps and significantly advance learning for all students is *human resources.* Leadership for learning involves high levels of skill in the allocation of human resources to achieve the shared vision. Key to the effective allocation of human resources is putting the interests of the student at the center. Effective management of *students* includes providing structure, motivation, and direction to ensure that their basic, social, and learning needs are met. Effective management of the *teaching staff* involves strength analysis, motivation, and allocation of staff to best address student needs. In addition, for teachers and staff to be effective, their basic, social, and learning needs must be met as well. Related and important human resource management skills include acquiring, motivating, and effectively using volunteer, parent, community, and district resources to advance equity and excellence in student learning.

Schools that advance equity and excellence in student learning put student learning needs at the center and design human resource allocation strategies to create learning environments that provide the best chances for students to be successful. This is most evident at the high school level. Two high schools that have put learning first are Elmont Memorial High School in Elmont, New York, and Jack Britt High School in Fayetteville, North Carolina. At Elmont, the administrative team had to do scheduling by hand because the scheduling software they had been using was designed to prioritize teacher preferences over student learning needs. The school wanted to design the schedule around student needs in order to maximize learning opportunities for students.

Similarly, Jack Britt High School schedules its students by developing a schedule that provides a mix of core and elective classes to ensure that students don't do poorly because they get bogged down one semester in heavy-demand classes only to have that be followed by a semester with all electives and limited academic demand.

Scheduling is clearly a critical factor in the allocation of human resources. Schools that put learning first seek ways to assign the most effective teachers to students who need the most help. This is consistent with the Education Trust's research on effective high schools that strategically design schedules around student needs rather than staff needs (Education Trust, 2005). They also allocate class sizes to advance equity and excellence in student learning and provide access for all students to high-level classes.

Management of human resources involves defining effective teaching practice and aligning elements of the human resource management system—recruitment, hiring, tenure, evaluation, professional development, compensation, and promotion—to support continually strengthening the teaching force (Heneman & Milanowski, 2004).

The human resources audit in Figure 7.4 provides critical information to enable further investigation and analysis of data regarding the centrality of student needs to the design of the human resource management system at the school. With these data in hand, the school can begin to identify areas for focused improvement.

As with financial resources management, the planning process for identifying interventions to address human resource management needs should be developed with explicit expectations or goals for improved student engagement and learning or other expected outcomes. These should be periodically reviewed, assessed, and compared to baseline data to evaluate progress and refine the plan for continuous improvement.

PHYSICAL RESOURCES

The third category of resources is the effective management of physical resources. The physical plant includes the physical surroundings of the school, such as the building and grounds, as well as the condition and use of classrooms; common areas such as the school entryway, the cafeteria, restrooms; and teacher spaces.

The goal of the physical space should be to address students' basic needs for safety and comfort, social needs such as opportunities for positive interaction with others, and learning needs such as adequate space for student engagement and learning. Figure 7.5 is an audit of physical resources that can be used to assess current conditions relating to the physical plant and its potential impact on students and others who use the school facility.

Figure 7.4   Audit Guide: Managing and Aligning Human Resources

---

Step 1: Understand the Baseline

What is the current distribution of school human resources?

- What human resources exist in your school, and how are they allocated? Include number, types, and experience levels of personnel allocated to departments, grade levels, courses (by ability level), extracurricular activities, and support services (clerical, food service, security, custodial, etc.).
- What human resources are available that are not reflected in the school budget? Consider business sponsorships, volunteers, parent and community organizations, and students.

Step 2: Examine Disaggregated Outcomes

What is the relationship between the allocation of resources and teaching and learning outcomes? Continue this analysis until you have a clear understanding of the gaps between the vision for resources targeted to student learning needs and the current reality (the vision gap).
For all schools, consider the following:

- What groups of students are achieving and what groups are failing?
- What human resources are allocated to achieving students? What resources are allocated to failing students? (Consider class sizes, allocation of experienced or effective teachers, academic enrichment programming, etc.)
- What remedial, behavioral, engagement, relationship building, language acquisition, and emotional support services are associated with improved student outcomes?

For middle and high schools, consider the following:

- What is the relationship between teacher allocation to courses and student learning outcomes?
- What groups of students are engaged, and what groups are not engaged?
- What financial and human resources are allocated to engaged students? What resources are allocated to students who are not engaged?

Step 3: Analyze Current Practices

Examine the current management and allocation of resources to promote growth in student learning.
For all schools, consider the following:

- How are human resources allocated to improve student achievement and engagement (through recruitment, hiring, professional development, leadership development, evaluation, compensation, and promotion)?
- Is there a process in place to expand and extend the current human resources to promote growth in student learning?

Step 4: Consider Common Problems in Allocating Resources That May Need to Be Addressed

- Does the vision for equity and excellence in student learning drive the use of human resources in the school?

- Is the allocation of teachers to courses designed to support teachers in strengthening their teaching practice and provide opportunities for all types of students to have access to the best teachers in the school?
- Are scheduling decisions made to maximize student opportunity for learning, including the following?
  o Distributing the most challenging courses so students can invest sufficient time in mastering course content
  o Ensuring students have supplemental support as needed to succeed in challenging courses
  o Ensuring that students have access and counseling to take courses that provide prerequisites needed for entrance to college
- Does student grouping for services result in segregation of students by race, background, or ability level?
- Are decisions about the allocation of resources based on maintaining job security and the status quo in order to minimize inconvenience to teachers?
- Is a regular process in place to assess the value added from resource investments?
- Is there a process in place to abandon past practices that do not target critical need areas and redirect resources to advance equity and excellence in student learning?
- Is there a process in place to identify and expose resource gaps and advocate for resources to address those gaps?

Step 5: Answer Summary Questions

- How have you aligned human resources to advance the vision of equity and excellence in the school or district?
- How have you acquired and managed human resources to address learning inequities in your school or district?
- How have you worked to ensure a safe and secure learning environment for students and staff?

The audit provides suggestions about the kinds of space issues that often arise in school facilities. As with the management and alignment of financial and human resources, the most important criteria for assessing facility adequacy and condition puts teaching and learning at the center. In general, is the facility supportive of best practices in instructional design? Is it welcoming and does it foster interaction and engagement of students and teachers in the school?

Since the leadership team of the school is unlikely to have training in facilities design, the answers to the questions in the audit will rely heavily on an assessment of school climate and teacher, student, and public perceptions about the quality, condition, and design of school facilities. Where guidelines for school facilities exist, they typically are developed as architectural design guidelines for new facilities or as a measure of typical facility design for schools that currently exist.

The allocation of classroom space for students is a good example. Square feet of instructional space per student, as determined by the existing U.S. infrastructure for schools, shows large variations across schools

Figure 7.5 Audit Guide: Managing and Aligning Physical Resources

---

Step 1: Understand the Baseline

What is the condition of critical spaces?

- Classrooms
  - Is there adequate space per student?
  - Are the classrooms well ventilated and comfortable?
  - Are the spaces flexible to enable whole-group and small-group instruction?
  - Are laboratory and other facilities (e.g., art rooms, science labs, whole- and small-group instructional space, music and band rooms, gym and locker rooms) adequate to ensure learning and participation opportunities for students?
- Lunchroom
  - Is the lunchroom large enough to support adequate break time?
  - Is it comfortable and safe?
  - Does it support a positive climate?
- Bathrooms
  - Are they clean and safe?
- Entrances
  - Do building entrances ensure a safe and welcoming environment for students, staff, and the public?
- Campus
  - Is the campus clean, safe, and in good condition?
  - Are there adequate playing fields?
  - Are there adequate large-group meeting spaces?

Step 2: Examine Disaggregated Outcomes

What is the relationship between the physical space and teaching and learning outcomes? Continue this analysis until you have a clear understanding of the gaps between the vision for resources targeted to student learning needs and the current reality (the vision gap).

Are the basic social and learning needs being met by the physical space?

- Basic Needs
  - Is the space safe, adequate, a comfortable temperature, and with good ventilation?
- Social Needs
  - Does the space provide an inviting, welcoming, and flexible environment to encourage positive human interaction? For example, what do classrooms look like?
  - Are there carpets, tables, things in the room and on the walls that are culturally relevant?
  - Does the space foster opportunities for social engagement and participation?
  - Is the culture of the school reflected in hall and classroom displays?
  - Are the transition spaces (playground, lunchrooms, gym, and the campus) similarly welcoming?
  - Is there a place where the whole school community can get together?
  - Are there spaces that support student engagement and social networks, such as band practice, places for people to meet with teachers, places for clubs to meet, field houses, and soccer fields?

- Learning Needs
  - o How are the facilities being used to address student learning and engagement?
  - o Is the physical environment tailored to specific learning needs?
  - o Is there differentiated space: art room, science labs, small group, and large group?
  - o Are there displays of student learning such as artwork, writing, awards, and other evidence of student learning?
  - o Are there computer labs, libraries, and spaces for teachers to collaborate and work together?
  - o Are there telephones or communication systems where parents can access information about the school and about their individual child's progress?
  - o Is the placement of rooms supportive of learning and collaboration?
  - o Are the spaces integrated so that they welcome all students and encourage participation of all students in high-level learning and teachers in high-level teaching?

Step 3: Analyze Current Practices

Examine the current physical space and consider how it contributes to growth in student learning.

- What are the policies, procedures, and practices in place that dictate use of space?
- What behavior management practices are in place to prevent bullying or unsafe behavior?
- What personnel are allocated to space, and what rules and procedures are in place during transitions (on the bus, inside and outside before and after school, during the lunch hour, and between classes) and during class to ensure a safe, secure environment?
- How does the school work to communicate a consistent symbolic message through the use of wall space, displays, and classroom design?
- What policies and practices are in place to manage the quality of space through custodial support, food service, teacher practice, and ongoing building and equipment maintenance needs?

Step 4: Consider Common Problems in Managing Physical Resources That May Need to Be Addressed

- Does the vision for advancing equity and excellence in student learning drive the use of physical resources in the school?
- Are all physical spaces safe and secure? Are there adequate security personnel, surveillance equipment, and controlled access to the school grounds and facilities?
- Does the space communicate a positive, student-centered culture and climate focused on advancing equity and excellence in student learning?
- Does the space clearly communicate the vision and learning objectives of the school and classrooms and provide a stake for every child through displays that celebrate their achievements, document their accomplishments, and recognize their unique contributions by reflecting student interests, heritage, and values?

Step 5: Answer Summary Questions

- How have you aligned all physical resources (facilities and equipment) to advance the vision of equity and excellence in the school or district?
- How have you acquired and managed physical resources to address learning inequities in your school or district?
- How have you worked to ensure a safe and secure learning environment for students and staff?

as well as regional variation. Having said that, the average in the United States is about 110 square feet per elementary student, 155 square feet per middle school student, and 160 square feet per high school student (Wohlers, 1995). Ideal class sizes for elementary students are smaller than for middle and high school students, so classroom size needs also vary by school level.

In addition to adequacy in terms of size, the physical space should address the basic social and learning needs of students. A critical element of this is to ensure that all students feel welcome and that the space design doesn't support or reinforce the segregation of students by race, culture, or ability. Ideally, every student should feel welcome in every corner of the school, and the artifacts that liven the walls should reflect the interests of the entire student body.

A safe environment is a critical precursor to learning, and the design and monitoring of physical space contribute significantly to perceived and actual safety of students and others. When the principal of Jack Britt High School wanted to make a statement about the quality and safety of the high school, he focused on making the bathrooms clean and safe. Bathrooms are often a barometer for the quality of the facility. If the bathrooms are clean and safe, it is likely that the facility will also be clean and safe.

With the audit and data analysis complete, the school can begin to develop a facilities plan. The plan can exist at multiple levels, including how teachers allocate and decorate space in their own classrooms, to school-level decisions about work spaces for teachers, to district and community level decisions about resource adequacy for changes to the physical plant.

As concerns arise about the school's physical resources, they can be addressed through an evidence-based plan. Baseline, interim, and long-term impact of changes can be measured and assessed and future changes reflected on. In addition, staffing of the space may be considered to assess the need for security guards and an adult presence to support a welcoming, safe school climate that is conducive to learning.

Together, the management of financial, human, and physical resources provides an important foundation for addressing the basic social and learning needs of the school and its community.

Building an Engaged Community

All learning occurs through experience and social inter-action, so in order to advance student learning, schools must create opportunities for teachers and other stakeholders to work, learn, and grow together. This chapter describes how socio-cognitive leaders advance student learning by building engaged communities, including communities of practice within the school, a strong sense of community among students and parents, and partnerships with external communities. Figure 8.1 provides an overview of the process of building an engaged community using socio-cognitive leadership.

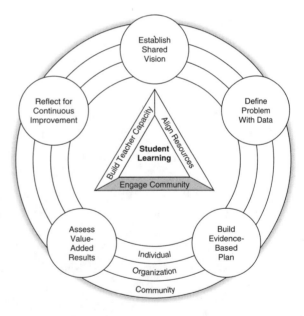

Broadly speaking, the term *community* describes the social relationships that support collective interests and contribute to the establishment of meaning and identity among community members. The challenge for school leaders in establishing learning communities therefore involves the following: (1) fostering relationships, (2) grounding the collective interest

Figure 8.1   Building an Engaged Community Through Socio-Cognitive Leadership

1. Begin with a clear shared vision of the preferred state: What will effective community engagement look like in the curricular and social context of this school?

2. Collaboratively, examine data on the community to assess vision gaps: What is the relationship between community engagement and teacher and student learning?

3. Develop evidence-based plans to build engaged communities: How can we build communities that best support student learning?

4. Examine student and teacher outcomes to assess community impact: How have teaching and learning improved as a result of the plan?

5. Consider areas for further improvement and build on successful strategies to continue to strengthen communities of teachers, students, parents, and other community members: How can we refine our strategy to continue to strengthen community engagement?

in a moral commitment to advance learning for all students, and (3) engaging school communities to advance student learning.

Building an engaged community requires focused work and attention to building relationships and a sense of trust among community members. The many principals we have worked with who have closed achievement gaps understand the importance of establishing a clear and consistent vision for the school and serving as a positive example for the school community. We begin our discussion of community by introducing an example of the efforts of a high school principal to build an engaged community committed to advancing equity and excellence in student learning. The case shows how Principal Alan Harris built relationships, grounded the community in a moral commitment to learning, and engaged the community in a collective vision so that they could move forward together. The case also illustrates the principal's skill as a leader in building trust to move forward.

Example: East High School

East High is a large urban high school in the Midwest. For 23 years, East was led by a legendary African American principal, Milton McPike. McPike had a way of bringing an increasingly diverse student body together and making students feel welcome and valued. McPike died recently from cancer, and he was profiled in a March 2008 article in the

Capital Times. The article quoted McPike from a 1992 interview where he said, "I've seen so much success through kids who everybody else has given up on."

He shared his secrets on building relationships with his students. "Put your arms around him, hug him, and say you look nice, but those are warm fuzzies. Do you want warm fuzzies? Hmm, mmm. Do I want warm fuzzies? Yep. Because sometimes we feel like we're out there all alone, and kids do too," he said (*Capital Times*, 2008).

When McPike retired in 2002, Madison Superintendent Art Rainwater called him the heart and soul of East High. During McPike's tenure as East's principal, East and McPike won several awards, including National High School of Excellence by the U.S. Department of Education, the Reader's Digest National Hero in Education award, and Educator of the Year.

Following his retirement, three principals moved through the building in rapid succession in one year while students, staff, and parents struggled to adjust to the change in leadership. At the end of the year, the district hired a young, energetic principal from a feeder middle school, Alan Harris, to assume the principalship at East.

Harris recognized the strengths of East High that included a history of strong community support, a cadre of high achieving students, and a student body and school community with a history of pride in the socioeconomic and racial diversity of the school. Despite these strengths, Harris also noted a community under stress due to the changes in school leadership, a significant achievement gap between African American and white students in the school, and a lack of minority student participation in the school's Advanced Placement and gifted and talented programming.

Harris's vision was to build on the strengths of the school a commitment to closing achievement gaps and advancing learning for all students. A dynamic speaker and talented presenter, Harris assembled data to share with the school community and build support for significant changes in curriculum and instruction to better support learning for all students. He moved to advance small learning communities and opportunities for access to challenging classes for all students at the freshman and sophomore levels, a change that had recently been implemented in one of the city's other high schools.

What he didn't realize was that the changes at the other school had mobilized and networked gifted and talented parents citywide, and they were ready with a strong and organized political opposition to his proposals, perceiving that investment in low-performing students would take resources away from the gifted and talented programming. In retrospect, Harris realized that he had not taken the time with parents to share the data and collaboratively build a shared vision of learning for all students, and he set about to develop this vision. By year two, the parents, who had successfully blocked school reforms through an end run to the school board, started the year with a more clear understanding of Harris's goals, a growing sense of trust in him—since he had listened to their concerns and agreed to slow down and bring them along with him in moving forward to address disparities in student achievement—and a commitment that the school needed to do something different to help low-achieving students succeed. Harris describes some of his work in building relationships to establish community:

(Continued)

(Continued)

When I was introduced to the parent community in May of 2005, they were understandably anxious about a third principal in one year. Meeting a room of more than 100 parents, I shared 50 things that I believe in to give them a sense of what values I lead from. From that came a desire to have a bimonthly contribution from me in the neighborhood newspaper. We now contribute to that newspaper and produce an enhanced bimonthly newsletter. What follows is my contribution to the neighborhood newspaper at the end of my first year where I shared what I learned in my first year. These communication tools have become an important aspect of building community support at the school.

What I have learned!

One year ago, I shared 50 belief statements in an effort to allow the East High community to know who I was as I joined the community. One year later, I'd like to share what I have learned about East High school, the students, the staff, and community. It is not intended to be an exhaustive list; in fact, it's a sampling. Hopefully, it sheds some light on what a dynamic and inspiring school East High is.

I have learned that each day at East High School there will be a student being tube fed with staff dedicated to the goal of that student's growth, development, and security when he leaves East High, and at the same time, there are students preparing for careers, students learning English for the first time, and students preparing to attend Harvard.

I have learned and am still learning about the depth of meaning of East Side Pride!

I have learned that when you meet a graduate from years past, they might break into the pep song, and I need to have it memorized.

I have learned that there are experiences such as math modeling and the Smokey's field trip that provide opportunities for students they would not find at another school in the country, including private schools.

I have learned that 30 out of every 100 students move in or move out of East every year.

I have learned that not only can you find purple ties, but also that they are often on sale.

I have learned that East High staff are brilliant, talented, caring, dedicated, and devoted to East High School.

I have learned that both students and parents want and expect very high standards.

I have learned that we have some problems to solve.

I have learned that our TAG [Talented and Gifted] students not only achieve at high levels, there is a culture of community support among them that is truly special.

I have learned what a PURGOLDER is.

I have learned that we have many students and parents who are not connected.

I have learned that we need three million dollars to renovate our theater so that the venue matches the talent that performs there every schoolyear.

I have learned that I have a lot to learn.

I have learned that we can get some great positive press about our kids.

I have learned that our kids believe East High's strength is diversity and tradition.

I have learned that our future is bright because so many people care about the kids at East High school.

It continues to be my honor and pleasure to be a part of the team at East High School, and we sincerely appreciate all of the community's support as we look forward to the 84th school year at East Side High School.

SOURCE: UW Madison Master Administrator Capstone Certificate Portfolio Document. Used with permission of Alan Harris.

For Alan Harris, building community means being authentic, listening to community concerns, and developing the trust, respect, common language, culture, and shared understandings that form the foundation of social relationships. Once these relationships are established in the context of a collective interest—in this case, a shared vision for advancing learning for all students—the community becomes a network that can be engaged to motivate, inform, develop, and invest (time, money, expertise, resources) to achieve that vision. Engagement sustains community by creating common experiences (successes and sometimes failures) that provide opportunities to strengthen friendships, trust, respect, language, culture, and understanding.

TEACHER COMMUNITIES THAT SUPPORT STUDENT LEARNING

Nearly 20 years ago, a researcher named Susan Rosenholtz (1991) studied diverse schools that produce high levels of student achievement compared to those that don't. She found consistent patterns: Compared to the *stuck schools*, the *moving schools* had shared goals, collaborative cultures, high levels of teacher learning, teacher efficacy, and teacher commitment.

Rosenholtz (1991) explains that shared goals provide the foundation for teacher collaboration:

. . . to the degree that teachers' everyday activity converges into a single harmony of organizational interests—underscoring what they should emphasize in teaching and how their success should be gauged—and to the extent that principals facilitate these everyday activities, teachers will come to identify those interests as their own instructional priorities. In particular, where teachers help principals define school goals and interact about how best to pursue them, where they determine school policies that facilitate that goal attainment, such as how students ought to behave, or help to socialize new recruits, teachers engage actively in constructing their school reality. Through these means school goals should come to be mutually shared. (p. 6)

In contrast, she notes,

. . . ambiguous goals, unclear, infrequent evaluation, and a lack of common purpose lead to greater instructional uncertainty and, at the same time, grant teachers wide latitude to define and independently pursue their own goals. In other words, [multiple and conflicting goals encourage] norms of self-reliance and, as a consequence, professional isolation from colleagues. The absence of professional interaction, of substantive dialogue about their work, carries profound implications: individuals may come to perceive that comparatively few colleagues suffer similar uncertainties about teaching, that they endure fewer instructional problems; and that if others experience few problems, there is embarrassment in admitting one's own. Thus, to protect their self-esteem in isolated settings, colleagues neither ask for nor expect any help, and cannot be imposed upon by others. In collaborative settings, on the contrary, teaching is defined as an inherently difficult undertaking; one that challenges the best of teachers. And if even the most capable teachers need help in similar situations, there is little reason to question one's own sense of professional worth. (p. 6)

When commitment to advancing learning for all students and a shared understanding of relevant practices to support that learning is internalized and shared by a community of teachers, teachers will seek collaboration. The interactions among teachers in this context create what Collins (2001) calls a flywheel effect that builds momentum and motivation to advance teaching practice. As Wenger (1998) describes, when a group of individuals work together to carry out a practice or focus of their work, it creates opportunities for advancing individual and group learning. This collaborative community of practice creates meaning in the work and shapes the way individuals view themselves and the role of their work in creating meaning for their lives. In essence, the community enables individuals to define their work as meaningful and to develop their own personal identity in relation to that work. Because teachers in communities of practice define themselves by their work in helping all children learn, they yearn for information on how to be more effective. Perceived barriers to collaboration melt away as teachers define their success as a person by their ability to grow. They continuously strive to reach that next challenging child and open up new worlds for him or her.

In this way, communities of practice are the engine that powers successful schools. They are fueled by core values and beliefs and nurtured by results. Communities of practice are supported by structures that facilitate communication (such as common planning time), but structures themselves are insufficient. The most effective communities emerge out of shared commitment to common goals and a belief that working together will advance the goals more effectively than working independently.

Communities of practice are comprised of three structural elements that shape participation and impact. Wenger (1998) describes them in the following way:

> The *domain* creates common ground and the sense of common identity. A well-defined domain legitimizes the community by affirming its purpose and value to members and other stakeholders. The domain inspires members to contribute and participate, guides their learning, and gives meaning to their actions.
>
> The *community* creates the social fabric of learning. A strong community fosters interactions and relationships based on mutual respect and trust. It encourages a willingness to share ideas, expose one's ignorance, ask difficult questions, and listen carefully.
>
> The *practice* is a set of frameworks, ideas, tools, information, styles, language, stories, and documents that community members share. . . . The practice is the specific knowledge the community develops, shares, and maintains. (pp. 28–29)

SOURCE: Wenger, E. (1998). *Communities of Practice: Learning, Meaning & Identity.* New York: Cambridge University Press. Reprinted with the permission of Cambridge University Press.

In a related body of work, Richard DuFour and his colleagues (DuFour, DuFour, Eaker, & Many, 2006) describe professional learning communities in schools, which are communities of practice whose domain is advancing learning for all students. Professional learning communities share the following characteristics:

- A commitment to learning for each student
- Collaborative teams whose members work interdependently to achieve common goals linked to the purpose of learning for all
- Collective inquiry into best practice and current reality
- An action orientation in which members move quickly to carry out actions to turn the vision into reality
- A commitment to continuous improvement
- A results orientation (pp. 3–5)

Socio-cognitive leadership captures and extends the concept of professional learning communities with its focus on the development of *communities of practice* that share a *common cognitive framework* for identifying and addressing important problems.

Socio-cognitive leadership builds the foundation for communities of practice among teachers by doing the following:

- Developing value and goal consensus through a collaboratively developed and widely shared vision for student learning
- Fostering social relationships that form the glue that holds communities of practice together
- Enabling teachers to create the building blocks of effective school practice by creating opportunities for teachers to do the following:
  o Analyze data
  o Examine evidence-based practices
  o Take risks
  o Assess results together to continuously improve teaching practice

To advance community, school leaders create a climate that supports relationship building, establish a shared vision of learning for all students, and engage the community to advance teaching and learning.

Establishing Relationships

Relationships form the glue that holds communities of practice together. Leaders support the development of positive relations through their example and by setting a tone of mutual support. They are socially intelligent leaders who build strong, positive relationships and have a strong sense of self-awareness and social awareness and exceptional skills in self-management and relationship management (Goleman, 2007). *Learning First* leaders also exercise transparency across communities, sharing core beliefs, values, vision, data, and goals (Bennis, Goleman, & O'Toole, 2008) to build community and foster trust, as Lisa Kvistad did as the incoming principal at Lowell Elementary.

Example: Lowell Elementary School

Lowell is a diverse urban elementary school in the Midwest. Lisa Kvistad became principal of Lowell in the Fall of 2006. Lowell was a strong performing, diverse elementary school, but following changes in leadership, the school community faltered. In this reflection, Principal Kvistad describes her efforts to build community as she assumed the leadership role in her new school.

Building community is all about inspiring confidence in Lowell School and in our changes in practice. As I began my principalship at Lowell, I knew there were different ways to do this—I invited community members in, and I also went out into the community. My "Coffee and Conversations" during the first weeks of school drew in some parents who were able to visit with me early in the morning around issues of decision making, discipline, and multiage. The assistant superintendent showed up at one of these meetings, and she was a perfect visitor to welcome to the group. I knew that the assistant superintendent had confidence in me to build and engage the Lowell community, and it was all I could think about during those first few weeks of school.

Those were some of my biggest tests of learning to build community—the days I'd buy coffee, juice, and breakfast sandwiches and meet parents for breakfast in their living rooms. Sometimes, we'd just sit and talk about family. Sometimes, I'd hold a younger sibling in my lap while a parent told me a heart-breaking story of school failure in the past. Many times, I'd visit with families while waiting with Lowell students at the bus stop. Some days I'd do three home visits before 7:30 a.m. I'd say hi to parents while they were still in their pajamas. We're all human—I think I wanted them to see me as human too. Last summer, I had a lunch bunch in the Darbo/Worthington neighborhood. I'd call and set a date with parents to take their child to lunch. I'd knock on the door and we'd chat about how summer was going and how everyone had grown by leaps and bounds. My favorite story is when I came to get a young man named DJ for lunch. His dad said to me, "Ms. Kvistad, you kept calling us last year telling us about DJ and his troubles. But you always said you weren't giving up on him. I believe you because now he's going into first grade, and he's doing real good." A look of true pride was all over DJ's face. We had a great lunch at McDonald's that day.

Building community within the Lowell staff meant bringing people together for professional development and focused work. I love staff meetings— I love seeing people working together; I love finding things to laugh about, and I enjoy hearing and telling the stories that make sense of the work we do. I always want staff meetings to give people a sense of place and a feeling of belonging to something that has the potential to change the lives of children.

To close this reflection, I have one more story that I will never forget. On one late afternoon just before winter break, a staff member came to my office to talk to me. We had a good conversation, and we were both looking forward to some time off to rest and reenergize. Before the teacher completely left my office she turned around, and I remember her saying to me, "I just want you to know . . . you have given me hope this year. . . . " I honestly can't even remember how I responded to her—I was so honored by her comment and humbled by the power of her words. I put my head on my desk and sat for a long time. She inspired me to keep going—and I realize that it is in small moments like these when community is truly built.

SOURCE: UW Madison Master Administrator Capstone Certificate Portfolio Document. Used with permission of Lisa Kvistad.

Through her leadership, her example, and her commitment to developing strong positive relationships with students, parents, and staff around a vision of learning for all students, Kvistad has healed and strengthened the relationships that form the foundation for professional community in her school. She provides an excellent example of socially intelligent leadership. As a leader, she has strong self- and social-awareness and exceptional self-management and relationship-management skills. These skills are perhaps most evident in transitions as leaders engage in interactions that build credibility, trust, and a sense of community.

ESTABLISH A SHARED VISION TO MOTIVATE AND GUIDE COMMUNITY ACTION

The social nature of learning and the centrality of community in advancing learning for all students are core values shared by schools that put learning first. The goal in developing a shared vision is to create a clear and strong focus on student learning as the chief priority for the school. The vision should be collaboratively developed and shared by all stakeholders and provide a compelling purpose and direction for the school, serving as a call to action for the school's stakeholders.

Many schools work hard to wordsmith a vision statement that they can point to on the wall, but for the schools that make quantum improvements in student learning, what is written on paper may be a useful reference, but what is written on the hearts and minds of the members of the school community is the real vision statement, the one that matters. It is that statement that is grounded in core beliefs and is collaboratively developed, shared, and reinforced.

So how do principals lead the development of these internalized value statements? They typically begin with core beliefs or values. Vision statements take on meaning when they connect with the core beliefs of individuals and reflect the hopes and dreams that led them to the profession and bring them back each day. Sometimes educators lose sight of these core values as they get lost in the reality of student discipline, angry parents, teacher lounge politics, scarce resources, poorly targeted professional development, and district decrees. But as the teacher told Principal Kvistad, strong leadership with a clear vision can give teachers hope and rekindle their connection with those core values that brought them to teaching in the first place.

Building a shared vision provides an opportunity to illuminate the hopes and dreams of the teaching staff and to engage in a meaningful conversation about where we are now compared to where we would like to be. Socio-cognitive leadership involves building on this collective vision by living it out in the examination of data to define current gaps between where we are and where we would like to be, by returning to the vision as a guiding principal for action, and by holding the school accountable for results, so failure to achieve the vision is a cause for action and not just complaint or concern.

Because the vision statement is developed from core values, it supports and reinforces building a sense of identity for individual teachers. This is who we are, and principled action flows from the core values that we have affirmed and committed to pursuing together. Thus, the shared vision becomes a yardstick for measuring progress and success and for holding one another accountable. It is internalized by all and it is tangible—it appears in stories about the successes and failures of the school, in individual and group goal setting and in both formal and informal planning processes.

DEFINE THE PROBLEM WITH DATA

Learning First leaders use qualitative and quantitative data to understand and build relationships that support improved student learning. They listen to students, teachers, and parents to understand the needs and values of the school community. Every social interaction is an opportunity to gather information about perceptions, concerns, and aspirations. *Learning First* leaders are hungry for social information because they know that learning is the product of social interaction. They engage in hundreds of daily conversations to understand, to model, and to advance a vision focused on student learning.

While these interactions often appear random, in reality, they are organized and systematic data gathering processes. *Learning First* leaders are outside in front of the school to greet children in the neighborhood and on school buses. They are skilled observers, interviewers, and listeners who continuously gather information and build relationships to engage the school community to support student learning. Regular observations, individual interviews, focus groups, surveys, community celebrations, and forums are the tools used to gather data and assess the health and status of the school learning community.

As we have shown, community engagement involves multiple communities located in various places within and outside the school walls. We have emphasized the role of the individual leader, communities of practice within the school, parents, and external partners. Figure 8.2 provides guiding questions for analysis of data related to building an engaged

Figure 8.2   Audit Guide: Building an Engaged Community

Step 1: Understand the Baseline

What is the nature of current community relationships and support, including the following?

- Student engagement
- Teacher collaboration
- Parent and caregiver involvement and support
- Community support

Step 2: Examine Disaggregated Outcomes

What is the relationship between community and teaching and learning outcomes? Continue this analysis until you have a clear understanding of the gaps between the vision for resources targeted to student learning needs and the current reality (the vision gap).

- Are students excited about learning?
- Are they active participants in learning?
- Do teachers collaborate to address problems related to student learning?
- What role do parents play in advancing student learning?
- Do parents feel welcome? Are expectations for parent support of student learning clearly communicated? Are data on growth in student learning shared with parents on a regular basis?
- Are parents in regular communication with teachers about their child's performance at school (negative and positive)?
- How is parent concern for children directed to advance student learning?

Step 3: Analyze Current Practices

Examine the current practices related to building an engaged community that supports advancing equity and excellence in student learning.

Student Engagement

- Are there positive, supportive relationships between students and adults in the school?
- Are there opportunities for students to find a home in the school (i.e., welcoming, socially and intellectually safe places where they feel willing to take risks)?

Teaching Community

- Who do teachers go to when they need to address problems of practice?
- What structural supports exist for developing communities of practice?
- What practices are shared?
- Are norms of membership made explicit?
- How is learning documented and shared?
- Are newcomers welcomed into communities of practice?

Parent and Community

- Is there regular, positive communication between school and external stakeholders?

Step 4: Consider Common Problems in Building an Engaged Community That May Need to Be Addressed

- Are parents of all backgrounds active participants in school functions (parent-teacher conferences, school events, PTA, school-site councils, etc.)?
- How does the school engage the broader community to support student learning?
- Does the school actively seek support and partner with community members to advance school and community goals?

Step 5: Answer Summary Questions

- How have you worked to understand the community and engage stakeholders in developing and attaining a vision of learning for all students?
- How have you developed internal and external relationships to engage, motivate, and support student learning?
- How have you served as an educational and student advocate in the community?

community. The audit focuses on collecting critical information for four areas of community engagement: student engagement, communities of practice, parents and caregivers, and other community stakeholders. Throughout, the focus is on assessing the personal connections between and among students, teachers, parents, and community members.

The audit information provides data for collaborative analysis to assess community relationships and identify areas that need to be strengthened to provide strong community support to advance student learning. Among the kinds of data that might be collected are social network data that ascertain the connections between students, teachers, parents, and community members. These data provide information to help understand how engaged and connected each of these groups is with the school community and help to identify individuals who are gatekeepers of information and resources within the school community. A social network analysis might ask each teacher to identify who they go to if they have a problem regarding reading or math instruction. This information can help school leaders understand what communities of practice exist within the school and consider ways to build relationships between teacher experts and other teachers who may need guidance in improving their instructional practice.

Once the communities of practice and networks are understood, the school can work to develop a plan to build, strengthen, and engage critical communities in advancing teaching and learning in the school. Baseline data regarding communities can then be used to identify ways in which the communities of practice intervention strategies have strengthened opportunities for communities to support student learning and where additional work is needed to build vital engaged communities.

Build an Evidence-Based Plan to Engage the Community to Advance Teaching and Learning

Having established a shared commitment to a common vision of learning for all students, the vision is reinforced by action. Early successes are celebrated and provide an opportunity to recommit to the vision. Decision processes are tied back to the vision and serve to reinforce and carry out the vision (e.g., Is this consistent with our vision? How does this advance learning for all students? Are there students we aren't reaching? What happened here? Why is this student's achievement level increasing at a slower rate than other students?).

By carrying out the socio-cognitive leadership process, the school community shares a commitment to advancing the vision. The collaborative work to define the problem and advance evidence-based solutions and then to use formative assessment to gauge progress all provides a common focus for the collaborative enterprise. Internal community is the engine that drives socio-cognitive leadership. An important structural support for establishing community within the school is to provide common planning time to enable teachers to build relationships, problem solve, and advance the vision together.

In addition, relationship building requires the ability to provide opportunities to connect on a personal level as well as a professional level. Investing in treats for meetings, providing time to check in and share struggles and successes, and making time to play together can provide important opportunities to establish trust, empathy, caring, creativity, and simply to enjoy one another's company—all critical glue that can hold the community together through challenges and disappointments, as well as energizing efforts that lead to successes.

With internal structures and supports in place, we turn next to evidence-based plans to engage school, family, and community partnerships.

SCHOOL, FAMILY, AND COMMUNITY PARTNERSHIPS

School, family, and community partnerships are critical to children's success in school. Families contribute to learning in so many ways:

- As tutors extending the teaching day and helping students master difficult concepts, supporting the completion of work, and extending learning time and opportunity
- As cheerleaders encouraging and motivating kids to apply themselves
- By providing complementary experiences that aid children's learning, such as by exposing children to ideas and experiences, and modeling behaviors that support learning

- By supporting and reinforcing teacher messages regarding appropriate behaviors, including reinforcing the importance of completing homework, applying themselves, and respecting school rules and teacher authority
- By instilling a belief in the value of education and a commitment to learning
- By supporting students in the logistics of education (getting kids to school on time, signing assignment notebooks and report cards, attending parent-teacher conferences, etc.)

Despite recognizing the importance of parent involvement in schools, many schools fail to engage this critical community. Joyce Epstein directs the Center on School, Family, and Community Partnerships at Johns Hopkins University. Epstein has conducted focused work on the importance and role of parents in advancing student learning for many years. Many of the *Learning First* schools we worked with relied on Epstein's work to guide the development of structures that support parent engagement in student learning. Her model identifies six characteristics of effective parent involvement:

1. *Parenting:* Home environments that support children as students, including parent education, family supports—such as health, nutrition, or other services—and home visits, particularly at transition points.

2. *Communicating:* Regular and effective school-to-home and home-to-school communications about school programs and children's progress, including parent-teacher conferences, translators, regularly scheduled information dissemination through notices, memos, phone calls, newsletters, or other communications.

3. *Volunteering:* Recruit and organize parent help and support through school and classroom volunteer programs, parent rooms or family center for volunteer work, meetings, and resources for families, and an annual time and talent survey.

4. *Learning at Home:* Share information and ideas with families about how to help with homework and other curriculum-related activities, decisions, and planning, such as information for families about the skills required for students in all subjects at each grade, homework policies and how to monitor and discuss schoolwork at home, and family participation in student goal setting and planning for college or work.

5. *Decision Making:* Include parents in school decisions and develop parent leaders and representatives, such as active PTA/PTO participation, advisory councils, parent advocacy groups, or committees for parent leadership and participation.

6. *Collaborating with Community:* Identify and integrate resources and services from the community to strengthen school programs, family practices, and student learning and development, including school-year and summer resources and activities related to community health, cultural, recreational, social support, and other programs and services.

Examples: Mendota Elementary and Wright Middle Schools

Mendota Elementary School has made parent and community partnerships a central part of their school improvement strategy. The principal, Sandy Gunderson, identified school community relations as a key challenge to student learning when she came to the school ten years ago. She and her staff invested heavily in developing strong ties to the diverse, low-income community that her school draws from. They have also worked with the nearby community center with parents using Joyce Epstein's parent engagement model and with local businesses to develop strong and supportive relationships that have produced good will, parental cooperation and support, financial support, and a strong cadre of volunteers to advance the work of the school. Throughout, Principal Gunderson and her staff have maintained a commitment to advancing the vision of high levels of achievement for all students and have worked with parent and community members to attain that vision. They credit community engagement as a key part of their successful strategy to turn the school around from an undesirable school to a model school in the community with all students learning to high levels.

CR   CR   CR

Wright Middle School, a charter school in Madison, Wisconsin, was established by the district primarily to address the learning needs of the low-income and African American community that neighbors the school. In the 2007–2008 school year, Wright celebrated its 10th year as a charter school in the community. In celebration of this milestone and in recognition of the social justice mission of the school, Principal Nancy Evans and her teachers decided to celebrate and study the life of James Wright, a community activist for whom the school was named. Principal Evans and her teachers used this celebration as an opportunity to orient the new sixth-grade class to the social justice mission of the school. During the year, the sixth-grade class studied the life of James Wright, the seventh-grade class studied his work, and the eighth-grade class studied his example as a social justice advocate. The school was redesigning itself to teach through thematic units and used this as an opportunity to transition to this new instructional approach.

As they learned more about James Wright, teachers and students alike became highly engaged in his story. One teacher took it upon herself to write a book about the life of James Wright, and another teacher wrote a play about his life and developed a drama course in which students studied drama and prepared to provide a public presentation of the play. The school used these events as an opportunity to strengthen their ties with the community by holding a ten-year celebration culminating in an open house with a presentation of the play and book to the public.

This community celebration advanced teachers' instructional practice and helped them develop a community of practice dedicated to advancing the thematic instruction and social justice initiatives of the school, engaged students in community activism and social justice, connected the school to its roots in the community, and engaged and invited the broader community to become familiar with the school.

SOURCE: Used with permission of Sandy Gunderson and Nancy Evans.

ASSESS VALUE-ADDED RESULTS AND REFLECT FOR CONTINUOUS IMPROVEMENT

The assessment of community communications, support, and involvement to promote student learning is continuous. Some schools use music programs, art, and student activities and athletics to build community both within and outside the school. Jack Britt High School ties student athletics directly to student learning. Players are students first, and coaches are teachers first. Student pep rallies are conducted to encourage winning on the athletic field and outperforming competitors on the state assessment. Participation in Saturday School and in student activities outside the regular school day is equally valued. Similarly, as students leave East High School each day, they are encouraged by Principal Alan Harris to "take the pride with you."

While formal assessments of organizational health or school climate may be helpful in assessing the strength of the community, human interaction is most commonly evaluated continuously by listening, observing, and tracking participation and support. Qualitative data, such as the story told by Principal Kvistad in the example on pages 124–125, provides clear evidence that the establishment of community is helping to build trust and reconnect teachers to their original goals in entering teaching. Other data that could be used to assess the value added in building community over time include the press coverage of the school, feedback from community members, measures of parent participation in parent-teacher conferences and other school events, voluntarism, effectiveness of community partnerships, assessment of the growth in student learning outcomes related to participation in after-school tutoring programs, student attitudes, behaviors and behavioral referrals, and donations to the school to support teaching and learning.

A valuable tool in assessing relationships between teachers and students is to conduct an audit of such relationships by posting student pictures and having teachers identify the students with whom they have developed meaningful relationships. The students not identified in this process are those that the school has failed to connect with in a meaningful, personal way. A similar activity could be conducted with staff to define the relationship networks that have been established in the school. This kind of mapping can inform focused efforts to engage staff as a community and to make sure that a strong, professional community supports all staff.

PART IV

Levers of Change

The Principal's Role in Advancing Leadership for Learning

Thus far, we have described socio-cognitive leadership or the idea that leaders in schools that close achievement gaps and advance learning for all students do so by establishing a cognitive decision-making framework that is shared throughout the school community. The socio-cognitive leadership framework includes five elements: a shared vision or preferred state, problem setting with data, an evidence-based plan, assessment of value-added results, and reflection for continuous improvement. This is the *what* of socio-cognitive leadership.

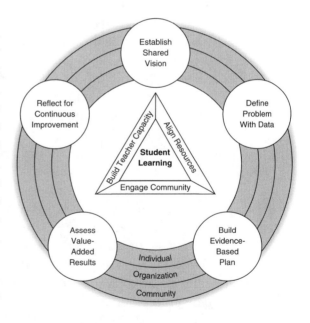

Socio-cognitive leaders use this decision-making model to advance four dimensions of leadership for learning: advancing equity and excellence in student learning, developing teacher capacity, managing and aligning resources, and building an engaged community. This is the *where* of socio-cognitive leadership.

In this chapter, we turn to a third piece of the puzzle and focus on *how* socio-cognitive leaders move schools. This chapter focuses on the individual, organizational, and systemic levers of change that define administrative mastery. Research on the decision making of expert educational leaders illuminates how expert or master educational leaders frame and address problems of practice (Leithwood & Steinbach, 1995). This research provides insight into the mind and skill set of the master administrator but does not provide an integrated dynamic conceptualization of leadership that advances student learning in the complex social context of the school organization.

Building on this work and the research on effective schools, Figure 9.1 depicts Levers of Change that principals can use to advance learning goals in effective schools.

The model begins with *setting a clear direction.* Research on motivation and leadership clearly suggests that the establishment of a clear vision provides a target that directs behavior and motivates individuals to work to achieve that vision. In this model, we emphasize a vision that is collaboratively developed and shared. Collaborative development of the vision is consistent with research on communities of practice and learning organizations that suggests that individuals are more likely to embrace a vision as their own if they had a hand in crafting it. Here, we suggest that vision should be collaboratively developed and shared among stakeholders. The vision includes a focus on improving student learning and advancing the school as a learning organization.

The development of a shared vision is critical to organizational change and implementation of educational reforms (Fullan, 2007; Honig, 2006; Leithwood & Louis, 2004; NSSE, 2003). By focusing the vision on advancing learning for all students, the principal directs attention and effort on advancing equity, overcoming barriers to success, and improving teaching and learning—the core mission of schools (Newmann & Associates, 1996). By focusing on enhancing the school as a learning organization, the vision directs attention to core processes that advance the school's capacity to succeed (Senge, 2006; Wenger, 1998).

The vision is enacted and refined through a series of purposive practices or levers of change that shape the experience of the school community. These levers include the ongoing development and refinement of the *individual leader,* the *organizational system,* and *external communities.*

At the *individual level,* the leader enacts and refines the vision through a clear sense of *moral purpose.* Clarity of moral purpose helps to shape leadership behavior and provides an inner sense of purpose and direction that motivates and sustains the principal and helps to motivate and shape the attitudes and behaviors of teachers, staff, students, parents, and community members (Sergiovanni, 2004, 2006). The shared sense of purpose

Figure 9.1 Comprehensive Leadership Development: A Model of Mastery in Principal Leadership for Learning

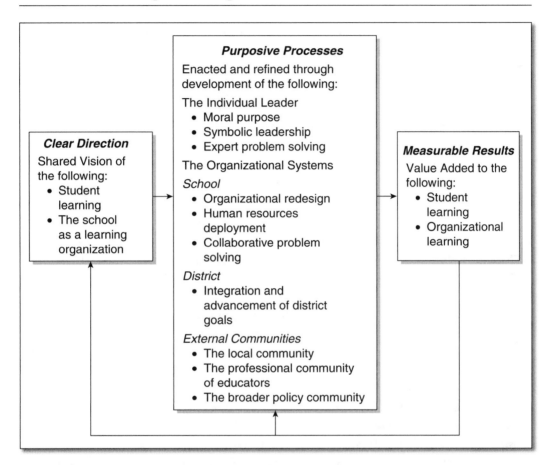

and direction is communicated both directly, through restatement of the vision, and indirectly, as the principal draws attention to the vision *symbolically* through storytelling, actions, behaviors, attitudes, and artifacts (Deal & Peterson, 2003).

Master principals are also *expert problem solvers*, able to adeptly navigate complex and difficult problems—what Leithwood, Begley, and Cousins (1994) characterize as "swampy" problems. Reviewing a series of studies on mastery in the principalship, Leithwood, Begley, and Cousins (1994) identify differences between expert and nonexpert principals in terms of the following:

- *Goals*: Expert principals adopt a broader range of goals and are more likely to value knowledge over feelings; they also see more complex connections between problems and their impact on student learning.
- *Principles and Values*: Expert principals are much more explicit about principles and values in their work.

- *Constraints*: Expert principals are more likely to believe that constraints in problem solving can be overcome.
- *Solution Processes*: Experts are more likely to engage in planning and consultation with others and view information gathering as a key problem-solving process.
- *Affect*: Expert principals are calmer in the process of problem solving.

In summary, expert problem solvers exhibit a higher degree of cognitive flexibility and a more sophisticated use of collaboration with others to identify and solve problems.

At the *organizational systems* level, expert principals leverage and influence *organizational structures and policies*. Consistent with an "open systems" concept (Scott, 2002), we conceptualize school organizations to have permeable boundaries and fluid membership, including staff on the school payroll, as well as a host of volunteers and stakeholders whose time and attention varies considerably at any single point in time. Individuals engage and disengage from the system for a variety of reasons depending on the decision locus and problem context. Thus, parents, extended family members, community members, researchers, district staff, policymakers, police, social workers, health care officials, and others may at any point in time be considered members of the school organization. Leadership mastery thus involves the ability to structure this amorphous and evolving community into *collaborative, problem-solving* communities of practice (Wenger, 1998) that are focused on problems of learning and are collaboratively engaged in developing organizational strategies and solutions to such problems (Sebring & Bryk, 2000).

Leaders do this by nurturing human resources and recognizing and aligning synergistic policies, structures, and supports that are mutually reinforcing and support the collaboratively developed and shared vision. Communities of practice work together to examine demographic, perceptual, achievement, and process or systems data (Bernhardt, 2004) and identify evidence-based interventions to address identified need areas (Slavin & Fashola, 1998; Wenger, 1998) and proceed to hold one another accountable for carrying out the vision (Elmore, 2004).

Beyond the internal workings of the school organization, systemic leadership involves recognizing and leveraging opportunities for broader systems to support student learning. Specifically, the principal leverages systems external to the school organization—such as *district* goals, policies, and resources—to advance school goals. In addition, the master principal helps to shape district vision, goals, and policies by sharing best practices with district leaders and developing, identifying, and supporting policy opportunities to advance learning for all students across the district.

Outside of the organizational system, the principal uses resources from and works to advance *external communities* helping members of these communities' individuals to recognize, share, and support the school's vision for student learning and broader learning community development. Members of these external communities include the following:

- *The local community* embodied in the neighborhood, school cachement area, the local community, including business and groups representing various community interests (Berg, Melaville, & Blank, 2006; Sebring & Bryk, 2000)
- *The professional community* through membership and participation in professional associations and opportunities to learn from, document, and share best practices with other educational professionals
- *The broader policy community* that could include helping to shape and provide feedback on policy adoption and reauthorization and providing broader leadership across the state, nation, and world

The principal guides the organization to achieve its vision by developing and sustaining the organization, by developing, implementing, adapting, or undermining external policies and pressures in order to advance *student learning* and *organizational learning.* The principal uses data to identify *measurable results* from school initiatives, examining implications for advancing learning for students and staff, focusing resources to address inequities in student learning, and advancing the school organization.

The model in Figure 9.1 paints a portrait of levers of change that reflects complex, advanced skills in educational leadership, drawing from a broad and deep skill set that advances organizational capacity and outcomes. We find that this portrait of the levers for change differs significantly from the view of the school as directed by a principal as manager.

In Figure 9.2, we position the principal as manager not as a straw man, but as the leader of the school rather than the leader of student learning. Many if not most principals have traditionally served this role in which their primary responsibility is to balance the needs of all members of the school community and to work to advance a positive image of the school among parents and community members. As part of their role in providing strong public relations for the school, they seek to keep abreast of current innovative practices in the field of education that they can adopt to support the school's image as a modern, innovative organization.

The principal treats staff members as professionals and approves requests from staff for professional development out of respect for the autonomy and professionalism of the teaching staff. The principal buffers and implements policy initiatives from the district or state as appropriate,

Figure 9.2 Levers for Change: A Comparison of the Roles of Principal as Manager Versus Principal as Socio-Cognitive Leader

Levers for Change	Manager	Socio-Cognitive Leader
The Individual Leader Moral Leadership	• Hears everyone's voice • Distributes resources equally among staff • Recognizes that not all children can achieve at high levels, so we must support them at the level at which they can succeed • Supports specially designed pullout programs, grouping • Holds high standards and expectations	• Offers unwavering public commitment to ensuring that all children are learning at the highest levels • Holds teachers accountable for ensuring that each individual child's learning needs are met • Commits to address cultural and structural barriers to student learning
Symbolic Leadership	• Manages impressions of the school • Believes that perception equals reality • Promotes the district and builds a positive image by publicizing/emphasizing successes and downplaying failures	• Accurately portrays school performance, and develop a sense of urgency for change by highlighting vision gaps in order to create dissatisfaction with the status quo • Creates a sense of hope, investment, and forward momentum in addressing vision gaps
Expert Problem Solving	• Continuously scans environment for innovative practice • Is highly aware and well informed of current best practices • Leads implementation of innovative practices	• Continuously scans environment for innovative practice that addresses the school's vision gaps • Adopts evidence-based practices to address critical gaps between the current reality and the vision • Pays attention to evidence that the practices have worked to address identified problems in schools with similar contexts
The Organizational System Organizational Structure	• Manages existing structures to meet student learning needs • Supports student learning by controlling assignment of students to leveled courses based on prior performance and limiting access to advanced courses to the best and brightest students	• Redesigns organizational structures to address vision gaps and ensure that all students learn • Examines barriers to student participation and success in highest level curriculum and redesigns structures to support access and learning of highest curriculum for *all* students

Human Resources	• Hires staff with strong teaching records and skills • Encourages teacher initiative by supporting teacher requests for professional development • Supports teacher preferences and norms for scheduling classes, such scheduling by seniority preference or by assigning the best and most experienced teachers to AP classes	• Hires staff with strong skills who share a commitment to the vision • Defines and focuses professional development based on teacher learning needs identified by student outcomes • Bases schedules and student assignments on student learning needs and priorities
Collaborative Problem Solving	• Structures teachers' time to allow for common planning time • Has teachers work together as needed to plan for changes in curriculum, alignment to standards, and so on	• Has teachers share a commitment to the vision and work together to problem solve and advance that vision • Engages teachers in student learning and working together regularly to solve challenging problems of daily practice and to scaffold student learning for success
District Support	• Implements district initiatives • Leverages district resources to support implementation of educational innovations • Manages district requests to minimize disruption (buffer) and for compliance	• Integrates and advances district goals • Uses district curriculum frameworks and planning processes • Seeks district support for data management, analysis, and collaboration and support in addressing vision gaps
The External Community The Local Community	• Seeks parent support for helping children succeed • Encourages parent participation in volunteering to support teachers in school activities, for PTO, and fundraising activities	• Communicates the vision and vision gaps to the local community to leverage support for change • Encourages parent participation to enable parents to understand school vision and help school achieve it
The Professional Community of Educators	• Believes the role of the education profession is to share information about educational innovations	• Believes the role of the education profession is to help educators link innovative solutions to identified problems and connect educators to others who have advanced student learning with specific leadership and reform strategies
The Broader Policy Community	• Believes policy shapes school action; school serves to buffer and implement external policies; leaders in school innovation share experiences with others through the policy community	• Believes policy informs school action; school integrates and adapts external policies to support efforts to address vision gaps; leaders in advancing student outcomes share experiences with others in the policy community

given the school context and history. The primary role is to keep the peace between potential volatile stakeholders, including students, parents, and staff.

We contrast this image of principal as manager to one of principal as socio-cognitive leader. The socio-cognitive leader puts student learning first. He or she courageously exposes inequities or inadequate student learning outcomes to internal (staff and students) and external (parents and community members) constituencies in order to ground the whole school community in a clear understanding of needed work around vision gaps. The goal is to balance a sense of urgency with a message of hope and renewal to motivate staff, students, and community members to work together to achieve the shared vision.

The socio-cognitive leader understands that the district plays an important role in providing data needed for analysis of the vision gap and data for value added analysis of program interventions. He or she strategically aligns district initiatives with the school's vision and seeks the support of the district in implementing changes designed to advance student learning.

As a result, the principal as socio-cognitive leader leverages individual, organizational, and external community support to advance organizational goals and move forward.

The District's Role in Advancing Leadership for Learning

S chools that put learning first have unique relationships with their districts. In general, three types of district and school relationships exist:

- Districts *impede* schools from putting learning first (but the school does it anyway).
- Districts *acknowledge and support* schools in putting learning first.
- Districts *lead* schools to put learning first.

Among the *Learning First* schools we have worked with, most operate in districts that fall into the first category, some fall into the second category, and a rare but lucky few fall into the third category (see also Simmons, 2006).

How and why do most districts impede school improvement? The primary reason is that there is typically no clear, shared vision in the district, so individuals within the district office and between the district office and the school work at cross purposes with one another. Districts without a clear direction act in response to environmental demands (political pressure from the board or community groups, emergent educational reform strategies, funding opportunities, individuals who champion particular issues or programs) rather than pursuing a specific vision or target. The most common example of this is that an effective, innovative strategy is blocked because it conflicts with goals someone else in the district is pursuing. Without a clear, shared vision, there are no clear benchmarks against which to judge new ideas, and reform initiatives become a political competition for scarce resources.

Among districts that acknowledge and support schools to put learning first, we see two primary strategies. First, districts support schools by creating effective structures and providing resources to support school improvement efforts. Often, there is a shared vision in the district, but it may be limited in scope or focus so that it is not sufficiently compelling, or there may be insufficient commitment to the vision for it to align systems at the district level or to drive innovation down to the classroom level. For example, a district goal for all third-grade students to read at grade level by 2012 is a clear, direct goal that can be communicated, shared, and supported, but it is primarily relevant to elementary school teachers through the third grade.

Furthermore, the vision becomes real when it is clearly communicated, compelling, shared, and creates a sense of discomfort with the status quo. Districts convince a weary and cynical workforce to buy in through their consistent focus on the vision. In addition, districts support school improvement by providing effective structures, materials, professional development, processes, and resources to support effective reform efforts. Districts that lead their schools to put learning first establish a clear curricular vision and put systems in place to support its implementation— recruitment and hiring, evaluation, school improvement processes, professional development, instructional frameworks, high-quality curriculum, and people, such as instructional coaches who can work in the classroom to implement the curricular vision and strengthen teaching practice. They develop and support formative assessment systems and create data warehouses that provide timely, accurate, accessible, and usefully displayed information about teaching and learning down to the individual student level. And they support the development of communities of practice among school leaders to share best practices and problem solve across schools, as well as within schools (Supovitz, 2006).

In the book *Breaking Through: Transforming Urban School Districts,* John Simmons (2006) laments the weak progress that districts have made in advancing student learning. He notes that in Chicago, which has made some progress in advancing student learning, high-gain schools complain that the district has been an impediment rather than an asset for their success. He suggests three organizing principles for district reform:

- *Consistency:* One vision in the classroom and the central office
- *Simultaneity:* Working everywhere at once (to align systems)
- *Quality:* Use of evidence-based practices and learning from the best (Simmons, 2006, p. 8)

In districts that lead reform, there is a clear and positive relationship between district-level leadership and the success of the schools. These districts use socio-cognitive leadership. They establish a clear vision or preferred state that is developed collaboratively with internal and external communities. They analyze and provide data to schools to set the problem and determine or help to determine the intervention strategies that individual schools or the district as a whole should pursue to address the identified problem(s). They hold themselves and their schools accountable for results measured against the vision, and they reflect for continual refinement, extension, and improvement of the plan for advancing student learning.

The Kennewick School District is a good example of a district that has successfully led its schools to close achievement gaps and significantly improve learning for all students.

Example: Kennewick School District

The Kennewick School District in Kennewick, Washington, is a district of about 15,000 students in southern Washington. The student population is 23% Hispanic and 73% Caucasian, with poverty levels ranging from 9% to 96% across the 21 schools in the district. In 1996, the district worked with the community and the teachers and principals to set a goal that 90% of third-grade students would read at the proficient level. At the time, third-grade students performed at about 70% proficiency districtwide, with significant variations across schools. The district received funding from the Gates foundation for their instructional focus and hired instructional coaches to support teacher development.

The district used socio-cognitive leadership to establish a widely shared vision of good teaching in which teaching lessons were expected to include a clear purpose, a high level of student engagement, rigorous materials, and measurable results in terms of improved student learning. The district developed data collection systems specific to the teacher and individual student to target instructional improvement strategies to the areas that needed it most.

In order to provide feedback to teachers to improve instruction and hold students, teachers, and schools accountable, the district mandated that all central office administrators spend 10 hours a week in the schools conducting walk-throughs and focusing on advancing instructional practice. The district provided instructional videos to develop and reinforce the vision of effective instructional practice and reinforce strategies for effective feedback. Today, individual schools and the district office remain committed to the 90% goal, and reading scores are consistently high across the district, fluctuating around 90% proficient.

SOURCE: Kennewick School District. From Lindbloom, M., Fancher, G., Rosier, P. (2007). "Quality Instruction Isn't Everything, It's the Only Thing," Presentation to the UW-Madison Wisconsin Idea Leadership Academy Conference, July 8–12. Used with permission.

Example: Madison Metropolitan School District

The Madison Metropolitan School District is an urban school district in Madison, Wisconsin. The district serves about 24,000 students in an economically and culturally diverse community. The district has developed a strategic framework to support student learning with a three-tiered focus on *engagement, learning,* and *relationships.* The school board has established a goal of all children learning to read at grade level by the third grade.

To support schools in achieving that goal, the district developed an educational framework that provides a vision for effective administration, teaching, and learning in the school district. A portion of the framework is reproduced in Figure 10.1.

Key features of the plan are to identify the three pillars of the strategic focus—engagement, learning, and relationships—and to define a shared understanding of how employees of the district and its schools will commit to the success of every child.

The district has also developed a balanced literacy framework, documented in a literacy handbook that provides clarity, common language, and definition to a districtwide curricular vision. The handbook provides guidance regarding evidence-based practices in literacy instruction and resources for teachers to advance their practice.

The district has also developed a sophisticated school improvement planning process designed in a five-year cycle. The district supplies schools with resources to support the planning process. The process is mandatory and includes a friendly observer visit to provide feedback and recommendations in areas for improvement that is grounded in achievement data as well as perceptual and process data collected at the school site. The annual principal evaluation process is related to the plan, and principals establish and are held accountable for annual evaluation goals related to plan implementation.

Figure 10.1   Madison Metropolitan School District Educational Framework

The Madison Metropolitan School District is committed to improving our capacity to carry out our strategic plan and reach our vision. Our educational framework describes our work to improve outcomes for students. It also provides a structure for organizing this work.

The framework is based on three fundamental concepts:

1. Student engagement, learning, and relationships are equally important.

2. Systematic, districtwide supports are critical.

3. A collaborative culture in which adults share responsibility for all students is essential.

To do our work, we will do the following:

- Use data to make decisions.
- Provide consistent systemwide interventions for each child who is struggling.
- Act on the understanding that each child may see the world differently than the adults in the school.
- Collaborate with one another to provide effective learning environments for all students.
- Establish and implement systems that respond to student behaviors in ways that promote positive change and re-engagement.
- Engage in professional development on research-based best practices.

The school improvement process guides schools through a comparison of their performance to the district vision, the board of education priorities, and the three fundamental concepts of the educational framework. Schools use this process to develop a plan for recommended changes, assess the results of these changes, and modify plans for improvement as necessary.

This process includes the following steps:

- Identify areas of strength and areas of concern through data analysis.
- Determine root causes.
- Select goals, objectives, strategies and timelines for improvements.
- Faithfully implement the plan.
- Assess outcomes through data analysis.

SOURCE: Used with permission of the Madison Metropolitan School District.

SOCIO-COGNITIVE LEADERSHIP AT THE DISTRICT LEVEL

Districts that put learning first use socio-cognitive leadership. Figure 10.2 on page 151 describes how districts use socio-cognitive leadership to lead reform efforts. First, district leadership works collaboratively with the school board, the community, parents, principals, teachers, and staff to define a shared vision of student learning to provide direction and accountability for action at the district and school levels. Internally, the district works with teachers and curricular leaders to develop an instructional vision that defines and illuminates strong instructional practice and establishes curricular coherence.

In addition to their work to see that the vision is carried out at the school level, districts that put learning first look to their own policies and procedures and hold themselves accountable for systemic alignment to the vision. These districts provide clarity and coherence through aligned policies in human resources management, data systems, and through symbolic acts that are aligned with the vision. For example, *Learning First* districts have a clear vision of effective teaching that is defined, documented, and shared among teachers. It is reinforced through an *aligned system of human resource management policies* that support the recruitment, hiring, evaluation, development, promotion, and use of teachers who meet the district's definition of effective teaching practice.

Second, *Learning First* districts support schools in accessing and analyzing data to set the problem. Data analysis occurs on a large scale at the district level, but the district also develops data warehousing capabilities that enable schools to access and analyze data at the school, grade, department, classroom, and individual student level. The district provides training to teachers and school leaders in data analysis and data-based decision making, and they model reliance on data analysis to understand and define problems. They have sophisticated data systems in place that collect student assessment data, demographic data, process data, and perceptual data. They provide resources to schools to enable them to implement formative assessment systems and support schools in learning to use data for decision making. They make data accessible in meaningful formats with a rapid turnaround and sufficient detail to be useful in directed school improvement efforts and provide professional development to teachers and other school leaders to analyze and accurately interpret data results.

Third, districts that put learning first select and support the selection of evidence-based plans to address the problem identified in the vision and data profiling phases of socio-cognitive leadership. They do this by providing guidance to schools in the types of programs that are proven interventions to address district goals and by encouraging schools to use evidence in the selection and evaluation of their own plans to advance the vision. A good example of the kinds of things that districts could do to advance evidence-based interventions is the Madison Metropolitan School District Literacy Notebook, which provides a clear evidence base for its recommendations on literacy instruction.

Fourth, districts hold themselves and their schools (leaders and staff) accountable for progress toward achieving the vision. They do this through the alignment of evaluation systems and school improvement planning processes to the vision. In Kennewick, district staff holds the schools accountable through their constant presence in the schools and by training district- and school-level leadership to provide consistent and high-quality feedback as they observe teaching practice.

Finally, *Learning First* districts engage in reflection to strengthen processes and outcomes and encourage and support reflection for continuous improvement at the school and classroom level through their design of improvement planning processes, professional development, and evaluation systems.

SOCIO-COGNITIVE LEADERSHIP AS SCHOOL IMPROVEMENT

We have developed two tools that we have used to build and assess socio-cognitive leadership in schools. Resource A is a rubric that principals have used to self-assess their leadership. Because socio-cognitive leadership requires a shared commitment to a common vision and collaborative work to carry out that vision, the highest levels of performance on the rubric—what we term *mastery*—involve significant engagement of the school community.

Resource B is a friendly observer-site-visit protocol that we have used to guide interviews and data collection to validate principal reflection on the

Figure 10.2 Socio-Cognitive Leadership at the District Level

Model of Socio-Cognitive Leadership in District Policy and Practice	Leadership Processes
Collaboratively build a shared vision or preferred state	• One vision in the classroom and the central office • Vision of student learning as the chief priority for the district and its schools • Includes a clear statement of the instructional vision • Creates a sense of dissatisfaction with the status quo • Creates energy for the district community to move forward together with a clear moral purpose
Support schools in accessing and analyzing data to set the problem	• All decisions are grounded in data • District designs a data warehouse to collect, manage, and disaggregate data • Data inform implementation of the vision • All instructional staff have access to the data and are trained to use it • District supports frequent formative assessment • Analysis of the data includes identification of trends, organizational strengths and weaknesses, projections, correlations, and emerging issues • Analysis includes comparisons to similar schools, benchmarking, and *value-added* evaluation
Support evidence-based plans consistent with the vision	• Goals of the plan are aligned to the vision, clearly specified, measurable, significantly challenging, and require the school to stretch to achieve them, yet they are attainable within a reasonable timeframe • Key leaders' responsibilities are clearly identified and include ways to mobilize others' talents • Resources are fully dedicated to the improvement strategies and additional resources are secured • Plans are flexible enough to be sensitive to local school context and identified problems • Baseline data are collected for future assessment of plan effectiveness
Hold district personnel and schools accountable for value-added results	• Expectations and consequences are clearly spelled out in advance; central office and schools are both held accountable for results • Schools set short-term and long-term goals in collaboration with central office personnel; results are assessed against these goals • Value-added assessment is used to improve teaching and learning; analysis of student learning needs includes a variety of assessment and evaluation measures beyond required state tests
Support and model reflection for continuous improvement	• Principal and teacher evaluations align with the vision and provide a concise but rich assessment of their role in the improvement effort, strengths, areas for improvement, possible changes, and next steps • District models reflection in answering the following questions: "How can I make this better? Where do I go next?" • District demonstrates a systems perspective by showing integration and connections among improvement efforts and takes specific steps toward continuous improvement for the district, school, and individual

rubric in Resource A. While the rubric and processes could be used for evaluative purposes, we consider them formative evaluation instruments to be used as feedback that can inform, guide, and strengthen leadership practice. The socio-cognitive leadership rubric can also be used as a foundation for a school improvement planning process or as a tool to shape conversations and professional development and to guide the development of a community of practice among principals within larger school districts.

CONCLUSIONS REGARDING THE DISTRICT ROLE

We have seen districts provide three types of support for schools in advancing leadership for learning: They support schools, they protect and buffer schools, and they use schools as incubators for ideas either by allowing opportunities for experimentation or by piloting district-level initiatives in targeted schools. Research suggests that organizations are innovative when they have sufficient organizational resources to enable them to experiment and try new things. Thus, districts can support innovation at the school level by maintaining innovation funds to support new endeavors.

In summary, socio-cognitive leadership can provide consistency in decision making that enables district, school, and community members to use the same intellectual processes and currency in evaluating alternatives and negotiating change. If district leaders use socio-cognitive leadership, school leaders understand that to obtain approval to move forward, they must show how their initiative relates to the shared vision of the district, how the problem it addresses is related to the vision and grounded in analysis of data, and what evidence they have that this initiative will address the problem that they have defined as a critical barrier to achieving the overall vision. Socio-cognitive leadership also facilitates rational decision making and a commitment to the vision rather than the political struggles over turf and the hierarchy that often characterize district leadership behavior.

By sharing a socio-cognitive leadership lens, together, districts and schools can act as partners pushing the envelope of teaching and learning, closing achievement gaps, and advancing learning for all students.

Resources

Resource A

Socio-Cognitive Leadership Rubric

Advancing Equity and Excellence in Student Learning

- How have you worked to help students who struggle?

- How have you worked to help students who are not challenged?

- How have you improved access to high-quality teaching and learning for more students?

Developing Teaching Capacity

- How have you worked to build teaching capacity to meet student needs and raise student achievement?

- How have you worked to build a professional learning community with high expectations and accountability for the improvement of teaching and learning?

- How have you worked to support *all* teachers, including teachers who struggle, to grow professionally and engage in reflective practice?

(Continued)

(Continued)

Dimensions of Leadership for Learning

Managing and Aligning Resources

- How have you aligned all resources (financial, human, and physical resources) to advance the vision of equity and excellence in the school or district?

- How have you acquired and managed resources to address learning inequities in your school or district?

- How have you worked to ensure a safe and secure learning environment for students and staff?

Building an Engaged Community

- How have you worked to understand the community and engage stakeholders in developing and attaining a vision of learning for all students?

- How have you developed internal and external relationships to engage, motivate, and support student learning?

- How have you served as an educational and student advocate in the community?

Directions: Apply the rubric separately to each of the four dimensions of leadership for learning on the previous page to assess socio-cognitive leadership. Ratings will vary depending on school context, principal skill, and leadership tenure in the target school.

Socio-Cognitive Leadership Indicator	Novice	Journey	Mastery
A. Shared vision of the preferred state Define desired results that align with overall school vision and lead to improved student learning.	• It is difficult to discern the chief priority of the school. • The vision does not fully define the purpose and direction for the school. • The vision is not well known or shared.	• The vision reflects a focus on student learning as one priority of the school among several others. • The vision describes multiple purposes and directions for the school. • The vision is developed and shared by most stakeholders.	• The vision reflects a clear and strong focus on student learning as the chief priority for the school. • The vision describes a compelling purpose and direction for the school and serves as a call to action for the school's stakeholders. • The vision is collaboratively developed and shared by all stakeholders.
B. Data-based problem setting Use multiple data sources and analyze quantitative and qualitative data to define learning gaps and needs.	• A limited amount of data is collected related to the key defining elements of the work of the school. • There is no meaningful disaggregation of data or tracking of trends over time. • Initial attempts at analyzing data are apparent but superficial. • There is no integration or synthesis of data.	• The system for managing data needs further development, but there is evidence of a systematic process for collecting data, and some data are disaggregated. • Analysis of the data leads to identification of the school's strengths, limitations, and emerging issues, but the data are not widely understood. • There is little integration or synthesis of data. • Communication of the data is limited and summaries of data are a snapshot of current conditions rather than a stimulus for continuous improvement.	• A comprehensive process for collecting, managing, and disaggregating data directly related to the vision and mission of the organization exists at all levels. • Analysis of the data includes identification of trends, organizational strengths and weaknesses, projections, correlations, and emerging issues. • The analysis includes comparisons to similar schools, benchmarking, and *value-added* evaluation. • The data are collaboratively reviewed to determine and revise and stimulate goals in the school improvement plan.

(Continued)

Socio-Cognitive Leadership Indicator	Novice	Journey	Mastery
C. Evidence-based plan Identify proven strategies to address identified problems and achieve the preferred state.	• Few goals and objectives are measurable, challenging, or attainable within a reasonable timeframe and are not directly focused on improving student learning or improvement. • There is limited use of research-based strategies. • Plans embrace innovation but do not address an identified vision gap. • Key leaders' responsibilities are vague and unclear. Inadequate resources have been provided. The timeline is unreasonable or not specified. • The means for evaluating the improvement strategies are insufficient to adequately assess the extent of the implementation and degree of effectiveness of the plan.	• Most of the goals and objectives are measurable, challenging, and attainable within a reasonable timeframe and are focused on improving student learning and/or improving organizational effectiveness. • Some of the strategies and action steps chosen to address the goals are research-based, validated strategies that address the identified vision gap. • Accountability responsibilities are not fully defined. Limited resources are provided, including professional development, materials, supplies, financial resources, and time. • An assessment plan does not fully address the means for evaluating and documenting baseline measures, growth, and the process of implementation.	• The goals and objectives work to meet the vision for student learning; are clearly specified, measurable, significantly challenging, and require the school to stretch to achieve them; yet they are attainable within a reasonable timeframe. • The strategies and comprehensive action steps chosen to address the goals come from research-based principles of high-performing systems with similar profiles and directly address the vision gap. • Key leaders' responsibilities are clearly identified and include ways to mobilize others' talents. Resources are fully dedicated to the improvement strategies, and additional resources are secured. • A systematic and comprehensive assessment plan for evaluating and documenting baseline measures, growth, and the process of implementation is in place.

Socio-Cognitive Leadership Indicator	Novice	Journey	Mastery
D. Value-added results Use data to track improvements related to student learning	• Little attempt is made to understand the results in relation to the school's beliefs and mission. • Limited attempts are made to involve parents, community members, or student representatives in defining the school's desired results for student learning. • The school improvement team does not identify perceived strengths or limitations of student learning. • A limited review of existing student assessment data is conducted. • Educational research findings and future trends are not taken into account in defining the desired results. • The statements of the desired results for student learning are vague and do not address meaningful schoolwide goals. • There is no evidence of an effort to establish priorities for the goals for student learning based on assessment data.	• A limited effort is made to ensure the alignment of the school's beliefs and mission with desired results for student learning. • The desired results for student learning are clearly stated, but they are not defined in terms of measurable goals or performance-based indicators. • Some of the desired results for student learning are not sufficiently challenging and/or do not address schoolwide expectations for student learning across the curriculum. • The analysis of student learning needs does not fully take into account the profile data and other assessment measures of student learning to determine desired results and priorities. • There is limited effort to determine stakeholders' perspectives on the strengths and weaknesses of student learning. • A planning or study team conducts a partial review of educational research findings and future trends.	• The desired results for student learning are directly aligned with the school's beliefs, mission, and vision. Each member of the faculty, staff, and administration can describe how the desired results for student learning are related to the school's vision. • A comprehensive data-collection process is used to establish baseline data in critical areas of student learning. • Value-added assessment is used by stakeholders to improve teaching and learning. The analysis of student learning needs includes a variety of assessment and evaluation measures beyond required state tests. • A thorough value-added analysis of student learning needs based on assessment results is conducted collaboratively by stakeholders. • Stakeholders conduct surveys and analyze stakeholder perspectives on the strengths and limitations of student learning and priorities for improvement.

(Continued)

(Continued)

Socio-Cognitive Leadership Indicator	Novice	Journey	Mastery
		• The process of establishing priorities for learning goals is guided to some extent by the analysis of learning needs.	• Study teams comprised of stakeholders review and share the latest educational findings, future trends, *user-inspired research*, and school reform models that have implications for defining desired results. • The school organization has identified three to five goals for student learning as priorities for the school improvement plan through a systematic data-driven decision-making process.
E. Reflection for continuous improvement Use analysis of results to inform future action.	• Plan provides limited assessment of roles in the improvement effort, strengths, areas for improvement, possible changes, and next steps. • Plan does not clearly address next steps or ways to improve. • Plan shows little understanding of integration and connections among improvement efforts. • Plan identifies few personal or organizational goals for continuous improvement.	• Plan provides an assessment that includes some description of roles in the improvement effort, strengths, areas for improvement, possible changes, and next steps. • Plan considers implications for equity and a nonsystematic look at evidence-based practice when answering, "How can I make this better?" and "Where do I go next?" • Plan shows some understanding of integration and connections among improvement efforts. • Plan identifies some personal or organizational goals for continuous improvement.	• Plan provides a concise but rich assessment of the role in the improvement effort, strengths, areas for improvement, possible changes, and next steps. • Plan models the values of equity, inquiry, and reflection when answering, "How can I make this better?" and "Where do I go next?" • Plan clearly demonstrates a systems perspective by showing integration and connections among improvement efforts and takes specific steps toward continuous improvement for the organization and as an individual.

Resource B

Learning First *Leadership Friendly Observer-Site-Visit Protocol*

Site-Visit Team Composition

Minimum of four team members, such as university representatives, principal colleagues, or mentors.

Sample Schedule

Dimensions	Learning	Teaching Capacity	Resources	Community
7:50–8:00	Team arrival	Team arrival	Team arrival	Team arrival
8:00–8:15	Site-visit team training	Site-visit team training	Site-visit team training	Site-visit team training
8:15–9:00	Principal overview	Principal overview	Principal overview	Principal overview
9:00–12:00	Individual or small-group interviews and classroom observations (Various according to dimension)	Individual or small-group interviews and classroom observations (Various according to dimension)	Individual or small-group interviews and classroom observations (Various according to dimension)	Individual or small-group interviews and classroom observations (Various according to dimension)

(Continued)

(Continued)

Dimensions	Learning	Teaching Capacity	Resources	Community
12:00–12:30	Lunch and observation or meeting with students	Lunch and observation or meeting with students	Lunch and observation or meeting with students	Lunch and observation or meeting with students
12:30–1:00	Additional interviews; opportunity to follow-up with principal	Additional interviews; opportunity to follow-up with principal	Additional interviews; opportunity to follow-up with principal	Additional interviews; opportunity to follow-up with principal
1:00–1:40	Site-visit team discussion	Site-visit team discussion	Site-visit team discussion	Site-visit team discussion
1:40–2:00	Principal feedback	Principal feedback	Principal feedback	Principal feedback

Site-Visit Goals and Procedural Guidelines

- Site team members will be asked to review portfolio of school data and principal summary and reflection prior to the site visit.
- The goal of the visit is to get a picture, in the context of the school, of the four dimensions of leadership for learning and how they are being carried out, and to provide useful feedback for moving school forward.
- The principal's overview should include the five areas of focus in the rubric: vision or preferred state, problem setting with data, evidence-based plan, value-added results, and reflection for continuous improvement.
- Interviews may be with individuals or small groups.
- Interviews may focus on informing a specific strategy the school is using to address the dimension.
- Separate interviews may be set up for each dimension, or team members could conduct an interview together if the interview informs more than one dimension.
- Interviews may be with teaching staff, students, administrators, parent volunteers, teacher leaders or coaches, union leadership—whoever can best inform the dimension and capture the leadership and the work of the school.
- Individual interview responses are kept confidential, although impressions and summary information about the results of the site visit will be shared with the principal.

- Typical interviews last about 25 to 30 minutes—enough time to capture how the school is addressing the dimension.
- Classroom observations are coupled with a short time to talk with instructors about the class; classroom observations can be with the whole group or with subsets of the team to illustrate a specific aspect of the work of the school.
- The principal's feedback includes an overview of the team's impressions. The goal is to provide additional written feedback follow-up after the site visit.

Site-Team Training

The site visit begins with a short 15-minute session with the team to establish common expectations and develop a shared understanding of the goals of the site visit. The training includes review and assignment of the four dimensions of leadership, a brief walk-through of the rubric (Resource A), and a distribution of the schedule and focus of the interviews. Example questions will be distributed for each dimension, and a classroom observation protocol will be shared. Objectives of the site visit are shared—specifically, that the site visit provides an opportunity to understand the principal's leadership and the work of the school in context. The goal is to provide meaningful feedback to the principal on his or her work in the school, to provide a clear sense of the team's impressions of the school's strengths and areas needing ongoing development.

Arm's-Length Relationship

Site visits are most productive when team members have an arm's-length relationship with the principal so they are not in a position to defend the principal or school but to provide constructive and honest feedback about the school as a positive, productive context for teaching and learning.

Expectations

Socio-cognitive leadership has two primary underlying principles. First, all learning is social, and the work of principals involves the creation of communities of practice that share a common cognitive framework for addressing problem solving. The framework implies that the work of the school is carried out collaboratively, and that the members of the school community (administrators, teachers, staff, students, and parents) share a common understanding and commitment to the vision, understand and can meaningfully discuss problems facing the school grounded in an analysis of data, share an understanding and are committed to successfully carrying out a plan for addressing identified problems and priorities, seek ways to understand the results measured in growth from a baseline measure, and participate in a reflective process that supports continuous improvement in teaching and learning in the school.

These expectations are spelled out clearly in the rubric. Of particular importance is the extent to which the vision, data profile, evidence-based plan, value-added results, and reflection are *shared*; decisions are *grounded in data*; plans are *evidence-based*; and results are measured as the *value added* by the school.

Dimensions of Leadership

Advancing Equity and Excellence in Student Learning

- How have you worked to help students who struggle?
- How have you worked to help students who are not challenged?
- How have you improved access to high-quality teaching and learning for more students?

Developing Teaching Capacity

- How have you worked to build teaching capacity to meet student needs and raise student achievement?
- How have you worked to build a professional learning community with high expectations and accountability for the improvement of teaching and learning?
- How have you worked to support *all* teachers, including teachers who struggle, to grow professionally and engage in reflective practice?

Managing and Aligning Resources

- How have you aligned all resources (financial, human, and physical resources) to advance the vision of equity and excellence in the school or district?
- How have you acquired and managed resources to address learning inequities in your school or district?
- How have you worked to ensure a safe and secure learning environment for students and staff?

Building an Engaged Community

- How have you worked to understand the community and engage stakeholders in developing and attaining a vision of learning for all students?

- How have you developed internal and external relationships to engage, motivate, and support student learning?
- How have you served as an educational and student advocate in the community?

Example Interview Questions

Team I: Advancing Equity and Excellence in Student Learning

Potential Interviewees: Principal/Assistant principal, school psychologist, counselor, teachers (regular and special education), instructional coach, classroom observation, parent, and student

Data: Equity audit (e.g., test scores, student placement, teacher assignment to classes, structure of classes, student engagement), with particular emphasis on learning outcomes for low income, minority, English language learners, gifted, and children with special needs

Possible Areas of Focus for Site-Visit Team: Inclusion, integration of children with special needs and special education teachers, scaffolding of learning and differentiated instruction, flexible grouping, discipline policies and outcomes, staff and student interactions (e.g., Do staff members know students by name? Do students greet adults in hallways?), integration of classrooms and interactions among students, participation of diverse students in advanced classes, evidence of challenging content for all students, and meaningful interventions in place to advance pace of student learning

Specific Attention to the Following:

Vision or Preferred State: What is the vision for advancing equity in student learning? How was it developed? How does it guide action? Is it shared by all? Do teachers and staff embrace it? Is it a call to action?

Problem Setting With Data: Is there a comprehensive process for collecting and analyzing data? What are the sources of data about instruction and student learning? Who collects the data? How are they used (at the classroom, team, grade, or school levels)? How does the school's leadership encourage or support the use of data? What types of data? What do the data suggest about the school's strengths and weaknesses? Can teachers articulate this?

Evidence-Based Plan: What is the plan? Does it emerge from the vision and from the analysis of data used to set the problem? What evidence supports the plan? Was effort made to observe the plan in a similar school or district? Are teachers committed to carrying out the plan? What resources has the school targeted toward plan implementation? Are they sufficient and appropriate? Are baseline data being collected to enable the school to assess the plan's effectiveness? Are the roles and responsibilities for plan implementation clearly specified and being carried out?

Value-Added Results: Can each member of the school community articulate how the desired results are related to the school's vision and how they will address the problem? Are results being assessed through value-added? Have a variety of forms of data been collected to assess plan effects? Are results collaboratively reviewed? Is there is a system in place to review the evolving evidence base to continue to advance school goals?

Reflection for Continuous Improvement: Is there shared reflection to reset goals, and inform future action? Is there attention to addressing systemic issues that impede goal achievement?

Team II: Developing Teaching Capacity

Potential Interviewees: Principal, teachers (regular and special education), Title I coordinator, individuals responsible for teacher professional development, teacher evaluation, instructional coaching, classroom observation

Data and Documentation: Curriculum models, teaming structure and practices, opportunities for formative assessment (teachers and students)

Possible Areas of Focus for Site-Visit Team: Use of curriculum models, coaching and learning opportunities for staff, hiring process, professional development, teacher teaming around curriculum content and lesson plans, problem solving, attention to addressing needs of low performing teachers, using and advancing learning of high performing teachers and all teachers, support for implementation of reform initiatives, school climate and professional accountability

Specific Attention to the Following:

Vision or Preferred State: What is the vision for developing and building an engaged community? How was it developed? How does it guide action? Is it shared by all? Do teachers and staff embrace it? Is it a call to action?

Problem Setting With Data: Is there a comprehensive process for collecting and analyzing data? What are the sources of data about teacher professional development? Who collects the data? How are they used (at the classroom, team, grade, or school levels)? How does the school's leadership encourage or support the use of data? What types of data? What do the data suggest about the school's strengths and weaknesses? Can teachers articulate this?

Evidence-Based Plan: What is the plan? Does it emerge from the vision and from the analysis of data used to set the problem? What evidence supports the plan? Was effort made to observe the plan in a similar school or district? Are teachers committed to carrying out the plan? What resources has the school targeted toward plan implementation? Are they sufficient and appropriate? Are baseline data being collected to enable the school to assess the plan's effectiveness? Are the roles and responsibilities for plan implementation clearly specified and being carried out?

Value-Added Results: Can each member of the school community articulate how the desired results are related to the school's vision and how they will address the problem? Are results being assessed through value-added results? Have a variety of forms of data been collected to assess plan effects? Are results collaboratively reviewed? Is there is a system in place to review the evolving evidence base to continue to advance school goals?

Reflection for Continuous Improvement: Is there shared reflection to reset goals and inform future action? Is there attention to addressing systemic issues that impede goal achievement?

Team III: Managing and Aligning Resources

Potential Interviewees: Principal; teachers (regular and special education); individuals responsible for financial, human, and physical resources of the school; security; school-linked services partners

Data and Documentation: Evidence of resource allocation, acquisition, and/or reallocation to support the vision for student learning

Possible Areas of Focus for Site-Visit Team:

Financial Resources: adequacy, allocation, acquisition, reallocation

Human Resources: development, management, building safety and management

Physical Resources: quality, efforts to maintain, use and adequacy for internal school activity, community outreach

Specific Attention to the Following:

Vision or Preferred State: What is the vision for resource management? How was it developed? How does it guide action? Is it shared by all? Do teachers and staff embrace it? Is it a call to action?

Problem Setting With Data: Is there a comprehensive process for collecting and analyzing data? What are the sources of data about teacher professional development? Who collects the data? How are they used (at the classroom, team, grade, or school levels)? How does the school's leadership encourage or support the use of data? What types of data? What do the data suggest about the school's strengths and weaknesses? Can teachers articulate this?

Evidence-Based Plan: What is the plan? Does it emerge from the vision and from the analysis of data used to set the problem? What evidence supports the plan? Was effort made to observe the plan in a similar school or district? Are teachers committed to carrying out the plan? What resources has the school targeted toward plan implementation? Are they sufficient and appropriate? Are baseline data being collected to enable the school to assess the plan's effectiveness? Are the roles and responsibilities for plan implementation clearly specified and being carried out?

Value-Added Results: Can each member of the school community articulate how the desired results are related to the school's vision and how they will address the problem? Are results being assessed through value-added results? Have a variety of forms of data been collected to assess plan effects? Are results collaboratively reviewed? Is there is a system in place to review the evolving evidence base to continue to advance school goals?

Reflection for Continuous Improvement: Is there shared reflection to reset goals and inform future action? Is there attention to addressing systemic issues that impede goal achievement?

Team IV: Building an Engaged Community

Potential Interviewees: Principal, teachers (regular and special education), team leaders/members (e.g., grade-level teams), parent leader and volunteer, students, external partners

Data and Documentation: Internal community, school-family partnerships (parent participation in conferences), relationship with union leadership, site council, district leadership, other initiatives, documentation of external partnerships

Possible Areas of Focus for Site-Visit Team: Membership in communities of practice, teacher teaming, sharing of curricular context and collaborative problem-solving, collaborative analysis of data, openness of teachers to welcome others into the classroom (teachers, parents, volunteers, paraprofessionals, coaches, etc.), teacher-parent partnerships, external partnerships that focus on advancing student learning, union role in advancing learning goals

Specific Attention to the Following:

Vision or Preferred State: What is the vision for building an engaged community as an active partner *in advancing student learning* within the school; with families, volunteers, and paraprofessionals; with external partners? How was it developed? How does it guide action? Is it shared by all? Do teachers and staff embrace it? Is it a call to action?

Problem Setting With Data: Is there a comprehensive process for collecting and analyzing data about internal, immediate external, and external community? What are the sources of data about professional learning community, parent participation, and external relationships (including school and district relations)? Who collects the data? How are they used (at the classroom, team, grade, or school levels)? How does the school's leadership encourage or support the use of data? What types of data? What do the data suggest about the school's strengths and weaknesses? Can teachers articulate this?

Evidence-Based Plan: What is the plan for building an engaged school community? Does it emerge from the vision and from the analysis of data used to set the problem? What evidence supports the plan? Was effort made to observe the plan in a similar school or district? Are teachers committed to carrying out the plan? What resources has the school targeted toward plan implementation? Are they sufficient and appropriate? Are baseline data being collected to enable the school to assess the plan's effectiveness? Are the roles and responsibilities for plan implementation clearly specified and being carried out?

Value-Added Results: Can each member of the school community artic-ulate how the desired results are related to the school's vision and how they will address the problem? Are results being assessed through value-added analysis? Have a variety of forms of data been collected to assess plan effects? Are results collaboratively reviewed? Is there is a system in place to review the evolving evidence base to continue to advance school goals?

Reflection for Continuous Improvement: Is there shared reflection to reset goals and inform future action? Is there attention to addressing systemic issues that impede goal achievement?

References

Argyris, C., & Schön, D. (1978). *Organizational learning: A theory of action perspective.* Reading, MA: Addison Wesley.

Arroyo, C. G. (2008, January). *The funding gap.* Washington, DC: The Education Trust.

ASCD and Northrup Grumman. (2007). *Introducing assessment for learning . . . and teaching: ASPIRE assessment system.* Retrieved January 30, 2008, from http://www.ascd.org/programs.aspx.

Bandura, A. (1976). *Social learning theory.* New York: Prentice Hall.

Bandura, A. (1997). *Self-Efficacy: The Exercise of Control.* New York: W. H. Freeman.

Bennis, W., Goleman, D., & O'Toole, J. (2008). *Transparency: How leaders create a culture of candor.* San Francisco: Jossey-Bass.

Berg, A. C., Melaville, A., & Blank, M. J. (2006). *Community and family engagement: Principals share what works.* Washington, DC: Coalition for Community Schools.

Bernhardt, V. L. (2004). *Data analysis for continuous school improvement.* Larchmont, NY: Eye on Education.

Bransford, J. D., Brown, A. L., & Cocking, R. R. (Eds.). (1999). *How people learn: Brain, mind, experience, and school.* Washington, DC: National Research Council.

Capital Times. (2008, March 31). *Former east high principal Milton McPike dies: McPike battled rare Adenocystic cancer.* Retrieved May 20, 2008, from http://www.channel3000.com/news/15746652/detail.html.

Chenoweth, K. (2007). *"It's being done": Academic success in unexpected schools.* Boston, MA: Harvard Education Press.

Collins, J. (2001). *Good to great: Why some companies make the leap . . . and others don't.* New York: HarperCollins Publishers.

Conrad, C. F., & Serlin, R .C. (2006). *The SAGE handbook for research in education: engaging ideas and enriching inquiry.* Thousand Oaks, CA: Sage.

Danielson, C. (2007). *Enhancing professional practice: A framework for teaching.* Association for Supervision and Curriculum Development.

Darling-Hammond, L. (2004). Inequality and the right to learn: Access to qualified teachers in California's public schools. *Teachers College Record, 106*(10), 1936–66.

Darling-Hammond, L. (2007). The flat earth and education: How America's commitment to equity will determine our future. *Educational Researcher, 36*(6), 318–334.

Darling-Hammond, L., & Bransford, J. (2005). *Preparing teachers for a changing world: What teachers should learn and be able to do.* San Francisco: Jossey-Bass.

Deal, T. E., & Peterson, K. D. (2003). *Shaping school culture: The heart of leadership.* San Francisco: Jossey-Bass.

Dewey, J. (1915). *The school and society.* Chicago: University of Chicago Press.

DuFour, R. P., DuFour, R. B., Eaker, R., & Many, T. (2006). *Learning by doing: A handbook for professional learning communities at work.* Bloomington, IN: Solution Tree.

DuFour, R. P., & Eaker, R. (1998). *Professional learning communities at work: Best practices for enhancing student achievement.* Bloomington, IN: Solution Tree.

DuFour, R. P., Eaker, R., & DuFour, R. D. (2008). *Revisiting professional learning communities at work: New insights for improving schools.* Bloomington, IN: Solution Tree.

Duncan, G. J., Brooks-Gunn, J., & Klebanov, P. K. (1994). Economic deprivation and early childhood development. *Child Development, 65*(2), 296–318.

Education Trust. (2005). *Gaining traction, gaining ground: How some high schools accelerate learning for struggling students.* Washington, DC: Author.

Elmore, R. F. (2004). *School reform from the inside out: Policy, practice, and performance.* Boston, MA: Harvard Educational Review.

Epstein, J. L. (2002). *School, family, and community partnerships: Preparing educators and improving schools.* Thousand Oaks, CA: Corwin.

Epstein, J. L., Sanders, M. G., Simon, B. S., Salinas, K. C., Jansorn, N. R., & Van Voorhis, F. L. (2002). *School, family, and community partnerships: Your handbook for action* (2nd ed.). Thousand Oaks, CA: Corwin.

Fitzsimmons, M. (1998). *Schoolwide behavior management systems.* Reston, VA: ERIC Clearinghouse on Disabilities and Gifted Education [ED417515].

Frattura, E., & Capper, C. (2007). *Leading for social justice: Transforming schools for all learners.* Thousand Oaks, CA: Corwin.

Fritz, R. (1996). *Corporate tides: The inescapable laws of organizational structure.* San Francisco: Berrett-Kohler.

Fullan, M. (2007). *The new meaning of educational change* (4th ed.). New York: Teachers College Press.

Goleman, D. (2007). *Social intelligence: The new science of human relationships.* New York: Bantam Books.

Hallinger, P. (2003). Leading educational change: Reflections on the practice of instructional and transformational leadership. *Cambridge Journal of Education, 33*(3), 329–352.

Halverson, R. (2004). Assessing, documenting, and communicating practical wisdom: The phronesis of school leadership practice. *American Journal of Education, 111*(1), 90–121.

Halverson, R., Grigg, J., Prichett, R., & Thomas, C. (2005). *The new instructional leadership: Creating data-driven instructional systems in schools* (WCER Working Paper No. 2005–9). Madison: University of Wisconsin–Madison, Wisconsin Center for Education Research. Retrieved August 17, 2008, from http://www.wcer.wisc.edu/publications/workingPapers/Working_Paper_No_2005_9.pdf.

Halverson, R., & Thomas, C. N. (2007). *The roles and practices of student services staff as Data-Driven Instructional Leaders.* (WCER Working Paper No. 2007–1). Madison: University of Wisconsin–Madison, Wisconsin Center for Education Research. Retrieved August 17, 2008 from http://www.wcer.wisc.edu/publications/workingPapers/papers.php.

Heneman, H. G., III, & Milanowski, A. T. (2004). Alignment of human resource practices and teacher performance competency. *Peabody Journal of Education, 79*(4), 108–125.

Honig, M. I. (2006). *New directions in educational policy implementation: Confronting complexity.* New York: State University of New York Press.

Jordan, H., Mendro, R., & Weerasinghe, D. (1997). *Teacher effects on longitudinal student achievement: A report on research in progress.* Paper presented at the CREATE annual conference, Indianapolis, IN. Retrieved October 1, 2008, from http://www.dallasisd.org/eval/research/articles/Jordan-Teacher-Effects-on-Longitudinal-Student-Achievement-1997.pdf.

Kelley, C. (1997). Teacher compensation and organization. *Educational Evaluation and Policy Analysis, 19*(1), 15–28.

Kozol, J. (1992). *Savage inequalities: Children in America's schools.* New York: Crown Publishers.

Kozol, J. (2005). *The shame of the nation: the restoration of apartheid schooling in America.* New York: Crown Publishers.

Lashway, L. (1997). *Leading with vision.* ERIC Clearinghouse on Educational Management. Eugene, OR: University of Oregon.

Leithwood, K., Begley, P. T., & Cousins, J. B. (1994). *Developing expert leadership for future schools.* New York: RoutledgeFalmer Press.

Leithwood, K., & Louis, K. S. (2004). *How leadership influences student learning.* New York: Wallace Foundation.

Leithwood, K., & Steinbach, R. (1995). *Expert problem solving: Evidence from school and district leaders.* New York: State University of New York Press.

Locke, E. A., & Latham, G. P. (1990). *A theory of goal setting and task performance.* Englewood Cliffs, NJ: Prentice Hall.

March, J. (1988). *Decisions and organizations.* New York: Basil Blackwell.

Maslow, A. H. (1943). Theory of human motivation. *Psychological Review, 50*(4), 370–396.

McKinley, M. L., Puma, A., & Witherow, K. (2006). Assessment tracking walls: A focus for professional dialogue. Draft for September/October Issue of *Orbit*, OISE/UT. Retrieved April 6, 2009, from http://www.hpedsb.on.ca/ec/services/cst/elementary/literacy/documents/MicrocsoftWord-AssessmentTrackingWall-Article.pdf

Miles, K. H., & Frank, S. (2007). *The strategic school: How to make the most of your school's people, time, and money.* Thousand Oaks, CA: Corwin.

National Center for Education Statistics. (2007). *Status and trends in the education of racial and ethnic minorities* (NCES 2007039). Retrieved from National Center for Education Statistics: http://nces.ed.gov/pubs2007/minoritytrends/

National Center for Education Statistics. (2007, December). *Highlights from PISA 2006: Performance of U.S. 15-year-old students in science and mathematics literacy in an international context.* Retrieved from National Center for Education Statistics: http://nces.ed.gov/pubsearch/pubsinfo.asp?pubid=2008016

National Study of School Evaluation. (2003). *Systemwide improvement: Focusing on student learning.* Schaumburg, IL: Author.

Newmann, F., & Associates. (1996). *Authentic achievement: Restructuring schools for intellectual quality.* San Francisco: Jossey-Bass.

Oakes, J. (1990). *Multiplying inequalities: The effects of race, social class, and tracking on opportunities to learn mathematics and science.* Santa Monica, CA: Rand Corporation.

Odden, A., & Archibald, S. (2001). *Reallocating resources: How to boost student achievement without asking for more.* Thousand Oaks, CA: Corwin.

Odden, A., & Archibald, S. (2008). *Doubling performance and finding the resources to do it.* Thousand Oaks, CA: Corwin.

Orfield, G. (2001). *Schools more separate: Consequences of a decade of resegregation.* Boston, MA: Civil Rights Project, Harvard University.

Rice, J. K. (2003). *Teacher quality: Understanding the effectiveness of teacher attributes.* Washington, DC: Economic Policy Institute.

Rosenholtz, S. J. (1991). *Teachers' workplace: the social organization of schools.* New York: Teachers College Press.

Rothstein, R. (2004). *Class and schools: Using social, economic, and educational reform to close the black-white achievement gap.* New York: Teachers College Press.

Sanders, W. L., & Rivers, J. C. (1996). *Cumulative and residual effects of teachers on future student academic achievement.* Research Progress Report. University of Tennessee Value-Added Research and Assessment Center, Knoxville, TN. Retrieved August 1, 2008, from http://www.mccsc.edu/~curriculum/cumu lative%20and%20residual%20effects%20of%20teachers.pdf.

Schulman, L. (2000). Taking learning seriously. In DeZure, D. (Ed.), *Learning from change: Landmarks in teaching and learning from Change Magazine, 1969–1999.* New York: Routledge.

Scott, R. W. (2002). *Organizations: Rational, natural, and open systems* (5th ed.). Englewood Cliffs, NJ: Prentice Hall.

Sebring, P. B., & Bryk, A. S. (2000). School leadership and the bottom line in Chicago. *Phi Delta Kappan, 81,* 440–443.

Senge, P. M. (2006). *The fifth discipline: The art & practice of the learning organization.* New York: Doubleday Business.

Sergiovanni, T. J. (2004). *Strengthening the heartbeat: Leading and learning together in schools.* San Francisco: Jossey-Bass.

Sergiovanni, T. J. (2006). *Rethinking leadership: A collection of articles.* Thousand Oaks, CA: Corwin.

Simmons, J. (2006). *Breaking through: Transforming urban school districts.* New York: Teachers College Press.

Slavin, R. E., & Fashola, O. S. (1998). *Show me the evidence: Proven and promising programs for America's schools.* Thousand Oaks, CA: Corwin.

Spillane, J. (2006). *Distributed leadership.* San Francisco: Jossey-Bass.

Sprick, R. (2009). Doing discipline differently. *Principal Leadership, 9*(5), pp. 18–22.

Starratt, R. J. (1995). *Leaders with vision: The quest for school renewal.* Thousand Oaks, CA: Corwin.

Staub, D., & Peck, C. (1995). What are the outcomes for nondisabled students? *Educational Leadership, 52,* 36–40.

Supovitz, J. A. (2006). The case for district-based reform: Leading, building, and sustaining school improvement. Cambridge, MA: Harvard Education Press.

Value Added Research Center. (2008). *The Chicago value-added project.* Retrieved October 21, 2008, from http://www.wcer.wisc.edu/projects/projects.php? project_num=371.

Vroom, V. (1995). *Work and motivation.* Revised Edition, Jossey-Bass Classics. San Francisco: Jossey Bass. (Originally published 1964).

Vygotsky, L. S., Cole, M., John-Steiner, V., Scribner, S., & Souberman, E. (1978). *Mind in Society: Development of Higher Psychological Processes.* Cambridge, MA: Harvard University Press.

Weiner, H. M. (2003). Effective inclusion: Professional development in the context of the classroom. *Teaching Exceptional Children, 35*(6), 12–18.

Wenger, E. (1998). *Communities of practice: Learning, meaning, & identity.* New York: Cambridge University Press.

Wenger, E., McDermott, R., & Snyder, W. M. (2002). *Cultivating communities of practice.* Boston, MA: Harvard Business School Press.

Wertsch, J. V. (1985). *Vygotsky and the social formation of mind.* Cambridge, MA: Harvard University Press.

Wohlers, A. (1995). *Gross square feet per student.* Council of Education Facility Planners, International Issue Track Brief. Retrieved August 18, 2008, from http://www.cefpi.org.

Index

CORWIN

A SAGE Company

The Corwin logo—a raven striding across an open book—represents the union of courage and learning. Corwin is committed to improving education for all learners by publishing books and other professional development resources for those serving the field of PreK–12 education. By providing practical, hands-on materials, Corwin continues to carry out the promise of its motto: **"Helping Educators Do Their Work Better."**